BLOODY DAWN

BLOODY
DAWN

THE CHRISTIANA RIOT
AND RACIAL VIOLENCE
IN THE ANTEBELLUM NORTH

Thomas P. Slaughter

Oxford University Press
New York   Oxford

Oxford University Press

Oxford   New York
Athens   Auckland   Bangkok   Bombay
Calcutta   Cape Town   Dar es Salaam   Delhi
Florence   Hong Kong   Istanbul   Karachi
Kuala Lumpur   Madras   Madrid   Melbourne
Mexico City   Nairobi   Paris   Singapore
Taipei   Tokyo   Toronto

and associated companies in
Berlin   Ibadan

Copyright © 1991 by Thomas P. Slaughter

Published by Oxford University Press, Inc.,
200 Madison Avenue, New York, New York 10016

First issued as an Oxford University Press paperback, 1994

Oxford is a registered trademark of Oxford University Press

Library of Congress Cataloging-in-Publication Data
Slaughter, Thomas P. (Thomas Paul)
Bloody Dawn: the Christiana riot and racial violence
in the antebellum North / Thomas P. Slaughter.
p. cm.   Includes bibliographical references and index.
ISBN 0-19-504633-1—ISBN 0-19-504634-X (pbk.)
1. Riots—Pennsylvania—Christiana—History—19th century.
2. Fugitive slaves—Pennsylvania—Christiana—History—19th century.
3. Violence—Pennsylvania—Christiana—History—19th century.
4. Christiana (Pa.)—Race relations.   5. Afro-Americans—
Pennsylvania—Christiana—History—19th century.   I. Title.
F159.C55S58   1991
974.8'15—dc20   90-22901   CIP

Printing (last digit): 9 8 7 6 5 4 3 2 1

Printed in the United States of America
on acid-free paper

This book is dedicated to the memory of
James E. Chaney, Andrew Goodman, and Michael H. Schwerner,
who died near Philadelphia, Mississippi, on June 21, 1964
—another tragedy in the ongoing story
about race, violence, and law.

Contents

Introduction

THIS BOOK TELLS THE STORY of a riot that erupted on September 11, 1851, at Christiana, Lancaster County, Pennsylvania, and of the people whose lives were changed forever by that violent event. Shortly after dawn on that day, Lancaster's African-American community rose up in arms against attempted enforcement of the Fugitive Slave Law of 1850; and, in the course of saving four men from the federal posse charged to re-enslave them, rioters killed the Maryland farmer who was trying to reclaim his human chattel.

Nine years before the War between the States, the events described in the following pages were proclaimed in screaming banner headlines that prophesied the bloody cataclysm to come. "CIVIL WAR, THE FIRST BLOW STRUCK," captured for many, especially in the South, the true meaning of what came to be known on both sides of the Mason-Dixon Line as the "Christiana Tragedy." The murder of Edward Gorsuch by men he claimed to own was not the only, the first, or the last death to result from the border warfare over fugitive slaves. The timing and circumstances of this particular riot were, however, of immense significance on the national scene.

Whether Americans could reach a rapprochement on the issue of slavery was not at all clear, and the Christiana Riot challenged the government's ability to mediate the demands of politics and law. The line between riot and rebellion was shifting during the antebellum period, leaving the definition of political crime open to broad construction. Federal prosecutors seized this imprecision in constitutional law to charge thirty-eight men on 117 separate counts of "levying war" against the government for their alleged roles in the Christiana Riot, making this the largest mass indictment for treason in the history of our nation.

Abolitionists, pro-slavery secessionists, and politically aware Americans in between those two poles anticipated the resulting trial as a test case for the Compromise of 1850. Some people in the South saw energetic enforcement of the new Fugitive Slave Law, which was one of eight parts of the intersectional compromise proposed by Senator Henry Clay, as a condition of their continuing loyalty to the Union. The previous federal law of 1793 provided no protection to alleged fugitives, no right to a jury trial or to testify in their own behalf. Unscrupulous kidnappers exploited the situation in a variety of ways, including taking free blacks by force and selling them into slavery on the pretense that they were fugitives. In response, as opposition to slavery grew in the North, some states passed personal-liberty laws designed to remedy abuses.

From the perspective of Southerners, the new laws went much too far, making it increasingly difficult for masters to locate and return fugitives who were their lawful property. Under one such law, Pennsylvania convicted Edward Prigg of kidnapping in 1837 for his actions in seizing a woman and her children and returning them to her Maryland owner. Prigg's lawyers appealed to the Supreme Court, which issued a complex decision in 1842 ruling the Pennsylvania anti-kidnapping law of 1826 unconstitutional, upholding the fugitive slave law of 1793, but declaring that enforcement was a federal responsibility. Pennsylvania, among other Northern states, vitiated the Court's decision in the *Prigg* case by passing new personal-liberty laws that barred the cooperation of state officials or the use of state jails for the holding of fugitive slaves.

As a consequence, Southerners still had a difficult time pursuing their escaped human chattel. The Fugitive Slave Law of 1850 was designed to alleviate that problem by putting the burden of proof on captured blacks, but giving them no legal power to prove their freedom. A claimant could bring an alleged fugitive before one of the new federal commissioners provided for by the law. In support of his case, the claimant could produce white witnesses or introduce an affidavit from a Southern court. If the commissioner decided in favor of the claimant, he received a ten-dollar fee; if he ruled in behalf of the alleged fugitive, his fee was five dollars. In either case, the costs of the slave-catching enterprise were drawn from the federal treasury.

The discrepancy in the fees was purportedly in recompense for the additional paperwork involved in remanding slaves, but anti-slavery advocates saw the additional five dollars as a bribe, which gave the commissioners a pecuniary stake in ruling against the alleged fugitives who already had the legal cards stacked against them. In fact, the Fugitive Slave Law did function in the slave-owners' behalf. During the first fifteen months that it was in force, eighty-four alleged fugitives were remanded South by commissioners, and only five were set free. Over the course of the decade, 332 African-Americans were enslaved under the provisions of this act, and only eleven were released by federal commissioners.[1]

The Union itself seemed to hinge on enforcement of this controversial law, and tensions were high in 1851 as both sides in the controversy over slavery tested how the Compromise would work. Armed resistance at Christiana to a federal marshal with a warrant issued under the new Fugitive Slave Law presented a challenge of immense political significance. In the eyes of pro-slavery Southerners, and ultimately of federal prosecutors, treason was the crime committed here, and the traitor was a white man named Castner Hanway, who allegedly directed the black mob in its attack on the federal posse. If the laws of the nation could be resisted with impunity, if citizens were free to "levy war" against the government as embodied in its legislative enactments and law-enforcement officials, then the very survival of the Union was at stake. Nothing less than conviction and execution of *white* abolitionist "leaders" would satisfy the honor of Edward Gorsuch's family, the State of Maryland, and Southerners who identified with the slain slave owner who died what they saw as a hero's death defending their rights under law. Nothing less than acquittal of all the rioters on all counts would appease the most radical abolitionists, who appealed to a higher law and a superior justice than that found in the Constitution and the Fugitive Slave Law of 1850.

So the lines were drawn in a fashion that pushed the Christiana Riot and the government's response to center stage in the national political drama. No other fugitive slave case, neither Jerry's in Syracuse nor those of Shadrach and Thomas Simms in Boston, had the same political significance at the time. Whatever the comparative importance of these other cases in law, whatever effect they had on firing the abolitionist movement and drawing the lines of conflict over the fugitive slave issue, no other fugitive episode struck the raw nerve of Southern honor so painfully or had the same impact on public opinion throughout the nation.

Indeed, no single event before John Brown's Raid contributed more to the decline of confidence in the nation's ability to resolve the controversy over slavery without wholesale resort to arms. Were we to search for parallels between the events leading up to the American Revolution, this nation's first civil war, the Christiana Riot corresponds in some respects to the Stamp Act crisis in the same way that John Brown's Raid does to the Boston Tea Party. Neither the Stamp Act resistance nor the

Christiana Riot caused the wars that followed them by nine years; however, each galvanized public opinion in ways that made it increasingly difficult to resolve differences amicably. Neither resulted in a decisive victory for law and order; indeed, each encouraged those who acted outside the law to think that they could do so with impunity. Both were later remembered by contemporaries as the beginning of a violent process that became a war.

Here the parallel ends. The Christiana Riot has not been treated by historians of the Civil War with the same regard accorded the Stamp Act crisis by the Revolution's chroniclers. It is seen more as a footnote than as a prologue to war. To the extent that the riot has had its historians, and it certainly has over the past century and a half, they have tended to focus on it for the dramatic qualities that its sources embody, for its significance as a local event, or for its contribution to the history of fugitive slave law. So the riot has its legions of local historians, its playwrights, its legal historians, and two compilers of documents who argue convincingly that the historical record speaks eloquently for itself. In all regards, these authors have served the memory of the Christiana Riot well. My purpose in retelling the story is not to correct or to supplant the contributions of other scholars and history buffs. Without them, this book would have been much more difficult to research. I am simply telling a story different from theirs.[2]

The setting and events selected for discussion here are less "typical" than they are illustrative of historical experiences in other places and at other times. I chose the Christiana Riot as a focus of analysis because it was the subject of attention in its own day. For that reason, the riot provides an opportunity to comprehend wider contexts of meaning. The politicians, political activists, newspaper writers, ministers, jurists, and literary figures of the time decided that these particular themes were important and that the historical setting depicted here was a significant one. I, drawing on their testimony and that of less historically articulate participants, have reinterpreted meaning for them, for me, and, I hope, for some of you.

At the time and since, this riot has been popularly known as the "Christiana Tragedy." The "tragedy" represents a white man's perspective that was not necessarily shared by all African-American participants. Incontestably, the riot was a tragedy for the family and friends of Edward Gorsuch, who died at the hands of his fugitive slaves. Just as certainly, officials of the State of Maryland and moderate pro-slavery Southerners throughout the region were horror-struck by both the riot and the outcome in the courts. The tragedy was felt by both Northern and Southern moderates who valued the rule of law and who prayed for the peaceful resolution of interregional tensions. Many—indeed most—abolitionists felt the tragedy to their cause and tried, unsuccessfully in the eyes of others, to disassociate their movement from the violence of the riot. The riot was a political tragedy for Pennsylvania moderates, the state's sitting Whig governor, and all those citizens who hoped to see the Commonwealth pursue a liberal course in the slavery controversy.

Perhaps least obvious, the riot was a tragedy for African-American residents of the region—if not for those who fled to Canada in the days immediately following the violence, and for men and women who sought to escape from slavery across the Maryland border. Free blacks and those who pursued their freedom were the victims of white Marylanders' vengeful rage, a general decline of faith in the rule of law, and an environment even more conducive to violence. White residents of Pennsylvania were even more suspicious, less sympathetic, and less tolerant of their black neighbors than they had been before. The racism, the poverty, and the other hardships associated with "free" black life were also parts of that continuing tragedy. The pains of dislocation were no less real for those rioters who found it necessary to abandon family and friends in order to avoid possible prosecution for what they saw as defensive acts. And the Civil War was no less a tragic outcome of the tensions exacerbated by the Christiana Riot, despite the positive consequences of that bloodbath.

The Christiana Riot is significant not just in its own right but also as a window on the culture of violence in the place where it occurred. The intense light of national interest in the case created a written record unsurpassed for its rich documentation of the perspectives of all parties to the ongoing struggle over slavery and race. The testimony of illiterate men and women recorded by newspaper reporters, lawyers, and court stenographers provides insight into a world normally lost to modern eyes. The commonplace thoughts of literate people, who were not normally prone to preserving their ideas about violence and race, are also revealing. This episode enabled Americans to articulate their fears in concrete terms, and they did so in voluminous detail.

A retelling of the Christiana Riot's story allows me to recapture some of the emotions that led to so much violence and to so many tears. It assists me in looking at the controversy over slavery as it was acted out in the lives of ordinary people, in watching them act under the stresses of an extraordinary event, and in comprehending better the perspectives of all sides in the controversy over ownership of other human beings.

The book looks more broadly at some of the ways that law functions as an expression of culture and how it represents the interests of some

groups against perceived threats posed by others. Sometimes the line between politics and law is unclear; the treason trial resulting from the
Christiana Riot is one such case. Law is always affected by social prejudices that are embodied in legislation and the actions of judges and juries.
Tolerance for particular kinds of violence, the presence or absence of
sympathy for victims, and the degree of identification with perpetrators
all play roles in communities' responses to violent acts. The riot helps me
to find additional meaning in the everyday actions of people, to discern
the motives that we do not normally examine thoughtfully in ourselves
and that we almost never explain.

The story told here illustrates some of the ways that sufferance of violence responds to broader social patterns. I explore connections between
physical brutality toward other humans and the way we define who really
belongs to our community and who does not—"us" and "them"—through
the example of one rural Pennsylvania county and the state and nation of
which it is a part. I use the Christiana Riot—including its short-term
background and causes and its immediate consequences—to illustrate these
themes, and I look at some of the same motifs in greater analytical detail
over the decades preceding the Civil War.

The story is about black participants in an ongoing battle for freedom,
and it is about the general problem of violence among different races and
classes and across gender lines. The book is about relations among people
and about perceptions they had of each other. It considers the meanings
of social, legal, and political relations within one county and across terri-
torial borders.

The poverty, racism, and savagery in my story are scourges that transcend the people, events, times, and places treated here. Some readers
will be saddened or angered or have their sensibilities irritated by the
violence portrayed in these pages. Some may detect the potential in this
book for an unpatriotically bleak interpretation of our national history.
Such readers could assert, quite rightly, that this is only a partial picture
of our collective past. It would be a mistake, however, to see the episodes
depicted here as exceptions to the ways in which we conduct public business. Only when we confront our national myths and begin to recognize
these truths can we realistically hope to achieve the sort of kinder, gentler
nation that we all wish we had. If this book has one goal, it is to play a
part in this process of owning our violent past.

BLOODY DAWN

Their story, yours, mine—it's what we all carry with us on this trip we take, and we owe it to each other to respect our stories and learn from them.

WILLIAM CARLOS WILLIAMS

So it has been for many of us—going back, way back, to the earliest of times, when men and women and children looked at one another, at the land, at the sky, at rivers and oceans, at mountains and deserts, at animals and plants, and wondered, as it is in our nature to do: what is all this that I see and hear and find unfolding before me? How shall I comprehend the life that is in me and around me? To do so, stories were constructed— and told, and remembered, and handed down over time, over the generations. Some stories—of persons, of places, of events— were called factual. Some stories were called "imaginative" or "fictional": in them, words were assembled in such a way that readers were treated to a narration of events and introduced to individuals whose words and deeds—well, struck home.

ROBERT COLES,
The Call of Stories: Teaching and the Moral Imagination

[1]

The Escape

EDWARD GORSUCH WAS A GOOD FARMER, and 1849 was a good year for his farm. By November, bacon, potatoes, and cider filled the basement for the winter. His slaves had put up jelly, preserves, and pickles in the pantry, where they also stored sweet potatoes and a keg of molasses. Gorsuch's forty or so cows (including the bull and several calves), fifty pigs (counting the shoats), thirty sheep, and uncounted ducks and chickens mooed, snorted, bleated, quacked, cackled, and crowed the prosperity of the farm. The dozen horses and six plows had done their season's work, and the corn house full of wheat (Figure 1.1) was a testament to the hard and successful labors of the animals and slaves who worked them.

Well, the granary had been full, but Gorsuch noticed that some wheat was missing and unaccounted for. It was not enough to be a serious financial loss or to affect the diet of the humans and animals for which Gorsuch was responsible as the patriarch of Retreat Farm in rural Baltimore County, Maryland, but as a careful husbandman, he made a mental note of the mystery. The lost grain could be a symptom of what might become a larger problem. The bin was about five bushels low, too much to be the quick work of rodents, and there was no evidence of a break-in by larger creatures. So the perpetrator or perpetrators of the robbery must have been human.[1]

Perhaps the slaves were obvious suspects. Most slaveholders of Gorsuch's day accepted petty thievery as a fact of life as unalterable as the weather. Indeed, there was a well-known ethic among slaves that "taking" from masters was not stealing in a moral sense. After all, if they were hungry or wanted for clothing and other essentials it was a consequence

FIGURE 1.1. The Gorsuch corn house *(with permission of the Lancaster County Historical Society)*

of masters' irresponsibility to their people. They were only using what was rightfully theirs; and what they took was only a pittance by comparison to what masters stole from them. As Frederick Douglass recalled from his youth as a Maryland slave,

> considering that my labor and person were the property of [my] Master . . . and that I was by him deprived of the necessaries of life—necessaries obtained by my own labor—it was easy to deduce the right to supply myself with what was my own. It was simply appropriating what was my own to use of my master, since the health and strength derived from such food were exerted in *his* service.[2]

Edward Gorsuch would have been surprised to find members of his slave "family" reasoning like Douglass or acting upon such logic. In his own eyes, Gorsuch fed his slaves well and was a kindly master. What is more, he had made provisions to free his slaves as each of them reached the age of twenty-eight years. He owned a total of twelve slaves, four of whom were adult males who plowed his fields and carried most of the heavy load of farm labor. Noah Buley and Joshua Hammond were in their early twenties. Later, after the tragedy, members of the Gorsuch family would describe Buley as a copper-colored mulatto with a "treacherous disposition." Nelson Ford and George Hammond each had eight or nine years left to serve Edward Gorsuch, who, according to the master's family, gave Ford only light work as a teamster because of his "delicate" physical condition. In 1849, Gorsuch thought his "boys" respected him; they certainly wanted for no essentials in his opinion, and their freedom was on the immediate horizon.[3]

Gorsuch was no Simon Legree. By all accounts, he did not beat his slaves. He tried to rule his household as a New Testament father, by love and mercy, seasoned, of course, with firmness and a dash of the Old Testament patriarch. To be sure, for the time and place in which he lived, Gorsuch had reason to see himself as a benevolent father, whose children—biological and legal, white and black, free and slave—should love and respect him for the character that he tried always to display among them. He was a man of honor and liberality in his own eyes and in the eyes of his neighbors, of his church, and of his sons. Neighbors brought him disputes to arbitrate because he was such a fair man. Gorsuch thought that his slaves saw him that way, too.

There was no law that dictated the manumitting of his slaves; there was no communal imperative that drove Gorsuch to make the financial sacrifice of freeing his chattel laborers. But, in retrospect, we cannot take at face value the master's testament to the unmixed humanitarian origins of his personal effort to gradually abolish slavery on his farm. After all, he did not free the slaves outright or offer them compensation for their labors in his behalf. What is more, there is good reason to believe that his moral concerns about slavery, which were certainly real, were fertilized by an economic calculation that many of his neighbors had already made. Gorsuch was not the first, or even among the first, in Baltimore County to see the light on this perplexing moral issue. In 1849, when Gorsuch's wheat disappeared, only 5 percent of northern Maryland's population was enslaved; and no other slave state had a comparable portion of free blacks within its borders.[4]

The ideology of the American Revolution, revivalism, and evangelical religion had certainly all played a role in this process of emancipation. Gorsuch's Quaker ancestry and Quaker neighbors perhaps also had some moral influence, as did the teachings of the liberal Methodist Episcopal Church, which he attended regularly and in which he was a "class leader." But given the timing and circumstances under which Gorsuch's slaves were to be freed, it seems clear that the movement away from tobacco production and toward the growing of wheat played a determinative role in the conclusion of Gorsuch and his neighbors that slaves were no longer a necessary, or even a financially desirable, feature of northern Maryland farming.[5]

The rhythms of tobacco production could keep slaves occupied throughout the seasons, while wheat called for intense labor at harvest but left little for a permanent work force to do the rest of the year. The keeping of animals and growing grain as a cash crop were not so labor-intensive that they justified slavery in economic terms, so Gorsuch really did not "need" his slaves in the same way that his ancestors had. But he could have sold the slaves South rather than setting them free. By 1840, 12 percent of Maryland's slave population ended up on the auction block per annum, many of them sold out of state. He might have kept some of the slaves, those he could use as agricultural laborers, and gotten rid of the others. Instead, he set his slaves free as they turned twenty-eight and offered them seasonal employment and a place to live if they wished to continue working on the farm. Some of them, at least, accepted the offer.[6]

Gorsuch was a good man, not a great one. He took what seemed at the time a responsible middle course, thereby failing, with the great mass of mankind, to transcend the evils of his day. Gorsuch was also a stubborn, foolhardy, and hot-tempered man, but such traits were no cause for celebrity in his own day any more than they are in ours. He also misjudged his slaves, repeatedly and with fatal consequences.

Gorsuches had, by 1849, lived and died on the land of rural Baltimore County for almost two hundred years. The original ten-thousand-acre grant had shrunk by subdivision over the generations, but the adjacent tracts of "Retreat" and "Retirement" in the far northern end of the county were still substantial working farms. Edward inherited Retreat, renamed for its historic role in the War of 1812, from his Uncle John in 1845. The heir was fifty years old when he came into his legacy, a mature man with five grown children. Rightly proud of his new status as patriarch of Retreat, he determined to manage the farm and slaves inherited from his uncle in a manner that sustained the honor and wealth of this substantial Southern family.

Gorsuch was among the larger slaveholders in Maryland. Only 10 percent of the state's slave owners held eight or more slaves. His farm was in the most prosperous agricultural region of the state, where the value of market produce in the twelve months preceding June 30, 1850, amounted to one and a half times that for the rest of Maryland. Laborers harvested twice as much hay in the region as in southern Maryland and the Eastern Shore combined. Northern Maryland, where the Gorsuches farmed, produced 70 percent of the rye and buckwheat and over half the oats and wheat grown in the state. The per-acre value of farms in the region was consequently higher than elsewhere in Maryland. So Edward Gorsuch was a prosperous farmer, indeed, and had good reason to be proud of the estate that he husbanded.[7]

FIGURE 1.2. Retreat Farm, home of the Gorsuches *(with permission of the Lancaster County Historical Society)*

The house in which Gorsuch and his wife lived on Retreat was partly constructed of logs, reflecting its frontier origins, but had been expanded by a stone addition from its original one and a half stories to three (Figure 1.2). The cellar windows still had the iron bars installed in a previous century to keep out the wolves and panthers that roamed the forests before the white settlers could eradicate such threats to a civilized landscape. The previous owner had added a number of outbuildings, including a sheep fold, ox stable, blacksmith shop, spring house, corn houses, hog house, and slave quarters. In 1841, he also built a brick-and-fieldstone barn, which resembled those in southeastern Pennsylvania constructed at about the same time.[8]

In November 1849, the barn was a busy place, full of life and the sounds, smells, and textures of people at work on a communal task. The farm's laborers—slave and free, women, men, and children, too—gathered each evening to cut and top the corn. Laboring in concert, the slaves blended elements of work and play. The harmony was that of work—muffled tones of sharp corn knives in the calloused hands of women whose lifetimes of experience made the tools extensions of their unconscious will—cutting and tearing the husks from the cobs, corn hitting corn as the ears were tossed to the finished pile. The older children, helping as befit their ages, were certainly less agile with the knives, more determined, more focused, working harder and accomplishing less than the adults.[9]

The melody was that of play—joking, singing, teasing, voices glad to be working at this task rather than others, pleased to see and feel and hear the rhythms of the agricultural cycle slowing to a more tranquil winter's pace. What songs did they sing, what jokes did they tell, what dreams did they dare to dream aloud for themselves and the toddlers around them? Almost certainly the walls echoed the old Maryland slave song "Round the Corn Sally," which provided a rhythmic accompaniment to the task at hand and articulated a not so subtle escape fantasy:

Five can't ketch me and ten can't hold me,
Ho . . . round the corn, Sally!
Round the corn, round the corn, round the corn, Sally!
Ho, ho, ho, round the corn, Sally!

With the seasonal change in the air, it was also a likely time for "The Winter," with its less cheerful metaphoric expression of the wish, the prayer, that the worst was over:

O the winter, O the winter, O the winter'll soon be over, children . . .
Tis Paul and Silas bound in chains, chains, chains,
And one did weep, and the other one did pray, other one did pray . . .
I turn my eyes towards the sky, sky,
And ask the Lord, Lord, for wings to fly.
O the winter, O the winter, O the winter'll soon be over, children . . .[10]

Perhaps they sang the hymn that expressed the dream—"We are Free"— which was a safe way to unburden the heart within earshot of the master. The younger children were surely playing against the tide of labor and song, climbing on the piles, exploring, testing the limits of their freedom, caught up in the festive spirit. But we must not exaggerate the joy or mistake the light-hearted banter for contentment.

There was also anger and concern and anticipation of unsettling change. But those were softer tones not heard, or at least not comprehended, by the master when he stuck in his head to see that all was well with his people, that the work proceeded apace, that the play was not interfering with the work that was the business of the farm. We do not know how often the still relatively new master of Retreat Farm checked on his employees and slaves as they labored in the barn. We cannot recover how his appearance affected the pace of work, the cacophony of sounds, or the joy of the task at hand. We do know that the slaves successfully hid what was in their hearts from the master as they went about their chores.

Occasionally, another sound would intrude: the low rumbling noise of wood on wood as male slaves rolled an ox cart full of unhusked corn across the floor and dumped it on the dwindling pile of work yet to be done. The dust raised by the crash was illumined during the day by light filtering through the door and the four large brick ventilators, one on each wall of the new barn. At night, and husking was principally an evening chore, lanterns would cast different, perhaps more haunting, shadows across the room. What did the male slaves talk about as they shoveled corn into the ox cart toward the end of this long work day? Perhaps we can guess, because they knew who took the missing wheat from Master Gorsuch's corn house, and they thought they were going to be caught. They were making plans for the dangerous, but exhilarating, new lives that they were about to begin.[11]

Rumor had it among the slaves that the master knew who took the grain. Nothing had been said yet, but they were waiting for the boot to drop. The miller had gotten suspicious when Abe Johnson, a free black man, offered to sell him five bushels of wheat. Johnson had no fields of his own, no obvious source for the grain. Johnson might have lied to the miller or declined to answer his question, but he trusted Elias Mathews, who was a Quaker, and told the white man the truth. The source for the wheat was several of Edward Gorsuch's slaves, Johnson told the miller. They brought the grain to him because "the person who had been in the habit of receiving from them had closed up"; in other words, this was not the first theft by the slaves. Their usual channel for disposing of stolen goods was unavailable, and they were forced to try something new. Perhaps they should not have trusted Abe Johnson. Johnson certainly misjudged Elias Mathews.[12]

No other information survives about the miller. If he agonized over the decision to betray the slaves to their master, it was an agony suffered in his heart, not one expressed on paper. If he shared the moral burden of other Quakers in the region, it could not have been an easy choice, and yet it was one consistent with the general character of Quaker relations with slaveholders in northern Maryland.

The Society of Friends, first in Philadelphia and then in London, had taken the lead in opposing slavery in America and the slave trade throughout the British Empire. Maryland Quakers, too, were influenced by the moral impulses that led the Philadelphia Yearly Meeting slowly, by stages, during the eighteenth century to renounce the ownership of other people. By the 1790s, the Baltimore Yearly Meeting had also effectively determined that no one could be a Quaker and an owner of slaves and tried its best during the first half of the nineteenth century to alleviate the worst suffering of African-Americans, slave and free, who lived in the neighborhood.[13]

To be sure, in the eyes of Quakers in London and Philadelphia, the Maryland Quakers could have done more. And in the course of a long and sometimes heated correspondence among the London, Philadelphia, and Baltimore Yearly Meetings, the Maryland Quakers tried to explain and defend the less strident stand they took in the movement to abolish slavery from the English-speaking world. "Our belief is," the Maryland Quakers wrote during the 1840s, "that unless we are careful to move under a lively sense of duty in each particular case, such is the extreme delicacy of the subject, that we are in danger of retarding instead of advancing the work of deliverance to this people."[14]

Their religious brethren would have to recognize that "the circumstances which surround us are peculiar, and our situation and difficulties are hardly to be appreciated by Friends at a distance." In their own eyes, they were not lukewarm on the issue, but their numbers were few and to unite with the Northern abolitionists, who *have* done injury to the cause," would be counterproductive. What is more, their concern for the souls of the masters, as well as the slaves, required that they maintain the confidence of the masters. To circulate abolitionist literature or take public stands against slavery in Maryland would, in the opinion of the Baltimore Quakers, be a mistake,

> *because* we think it would have a tendency to lessen our future usefulness and would probably close the door of access we now have to the slave-holders, who know we oppose slavery on conscientious grounds, that we have not selfish views in our opposition, that we are lovers of peace and that we are friends both of the master and the slave.[15]

For the Quaker miller Elias Mathews to collude with Abe Johnson and the slaves at Retreat would be a breach of faith with Gorsuch and other slaveholders in the region. Not only would he risk losing the white-men's business—and perhaps that was his greatest concern—but he would sacrifice any influence that he had with the owners of slaves and be less effective in efforts to assist the black inhabitants of the neighborhood. The fact that Johnson trusted the miller with his story suggests that Mathews was known to be sympathetic to the blacks and had treated them honestly and with regard in the past. But Johnson expected too much from the white man. He asked for more than a Quaker in northern Baltimore County was likely to do for a black. He was asking the miller to stand alone in opposition to the moral standards of the white community. Like Edward Gorsuch, Elias Mathews was a good man, not a great one.

As Gorsuch told the story:

The miller immediately called to see me and gave me the . . . information. I went with him to see the wheat, and believed it to be mine it perfectly corresponding with some that I had just before in my granary, and of which I had missed a quantity. I said nothing to my coloured boys about it but had a state warrant issued for said Abraham Johnston [*sic*], but Johnston finding out that they were after him secreted himself for a few days.

So the whites were looking for the free black man who could implicate Gorsuch's "boys" and assumed, wrongly, that the slaves did not know what was going on. In fact, the slaves were probably hiding Johnson, while making their own plans for what to do next.[16]

It was November 6, 1849. Noah Buley, Nelson Ford, and George and Joshua Hammond talked quietly, and no doubt nervously, as they shoveled corn into the ox cart. One of them casually asked a white carpenter who worked on the farm whether "the Boss is going to husk corn tonight?" Another one announced a bit more publicly than was normal or necessary that he was setting his rabbit trap before sunset, because it was "going to be a very dark night." Having done their best to act "normal," under cover of that very dark evening the four male slaves escaped through a skylight in the back building, climbed down a ladder, and sneaked away from the farm. We cannot know whether they ran simply because they feared the consequences of being discovered as thieves or whether stealing the grain was to raise money for an escape that they had planned all along. But run they did, with the help of Alexander Scott, "a tall yellow fellow," who was also one of Gorsuch's slaves. According to a black resident of Lancaster County interviewed long after the fact, Scott said that he brought Buley, Ford, and the two Hammonds in a wagon to Baltimore, where he put them on a northbound train.[17]

Another account indicated that the fugitives fled on foot, using the York Road as their path to freedom. This is much more likely than the other story, because four black men could not board a northbound train in Baltimore city without some challenge by local authorities. As William Still reported in his first-person narrative of Underground Railroad experiences:

Baltimore used to be in the days of Slavery one of the most difficult places in the South for even free colored people to get away from much more for slaves. The rule forbade any colored person leaving there by rail road or steamboat, without such applicant had been weighed, measured, and then given a bond signed by unquestionable signatures, well known.[18]

So the Baltimore train story was undoubtedly a ruse. There were good reasons to be cagey about the methods and directions of escaped slaves in flight. Circulating two contradictory stories about the route they took was one way of keeping opportunities open for those who might flee on another day. Stories told later, long after the event, still reflected the necessity, and the habit, of such deception. Descendants of the master believed into the twentieth century that the four slaves left on foot; while the oral tradition among local blacks still maintained that the men rode the above-ground railroad to freedom.[19]

In any event, such diversions were apparently unnecessary in this particular case, because Gorsuch never suspected that his "people" would run away. No special provisions were made to secure the slaves in their quarters. The master was shocked and his pride wounded the next morning when his son Dickinson shouted up the stairs that "the boys are all gone." Gorsuch blamed the free black man Johnson for enticing the slaves and deluding them with false hopes about the nature of life across the Pennsylvania border to the north.[20]

Free blacks were indeed a thorn in the side of Maryland's slave owners. As a foreign traveler observed in the 1790s, "house robberies are frequent in Maryland. . . . The judges attribute the multiplicity of robberies to the free negroes, who are very numerous in the state." A series of laws during the nineteenth century was intended to control the free black population, denying them the right to own dogs or firearms or to purchase liquor or ammunition without a special license. Free blacks were supposed to secure written certification of ownership before selling tobacco, grain, or meat. Nonetheless, the white community continued to feel plagued by thefts, which they blamed on free blacks. Whites did make one special exception to the rule against slaves testifying in court: in the cases of free blacks accused of stealing, slaves could give witness *against* them. Still, the stealing continued. By 1850, free blacks represented about 13 percent of the county population but a little more than one-third of those incarcerated in Baltimore's jail.[21]

The free blacks were not only thieves, according to Maryland's whites, but burdens on society in a host of other ways as well. They lived on the economic fringes, as the seasonal fluctuations of black men, women, and children in the county's almshouse attest. These free blacks also stood as models of an alternative life for the slaves. They were, in the eyes of whites, tutors in crime, receivers of stolen goods, and "kidnappers" of slaves. They lent their "free" papers to slaves, who sought the short-term liberty to travel the countryside visiting relatives or friends. They cajoled, goaded, and tricked slaves into lives of crime; or, worse yet, they misled them into believing that there was a better life for them outside their masters' farms.

In 1790, Maryland had the second largest free black population in the country; by 1810 it was first, where it remained until Emancipation. By 1850, seven out of every ten Baltimore County blacks were free; ten years later only one-quarter of the county's black population was enslaved. This had happened despite the efforts of slave owners to prohibit immigration of free blacks from outside the state and despite adequate numbers of proletarian whites in the city to carry the burden of free labor on their backs. The mushrooming of the free black population occurred in the face of laws restricting the movement and activities of free blacks, laws which proved impotent against the tide of black crime that whites saw as the consequence of black freedom.[22]

The whites tried laws that mandated the incarceration and sale of "idle" blacks into temporary servitude, banished from the state free blacks convicted of crime, and tightened the rules for manumitting slaves. The legislature regulated the times and conditions for worship services attended by free blacks, made it a felony for them to seek or possess abolitionist literature, and relaxed the normal laws relating to search and seizure to permit authorities freer access to their homes. On a number of occasions throughout the years, the assembly saw fit to restate the rule that no court of law could accept the testimony of blacks against a white person for any reason or pertaining to any crime. Better to let a white murderer go free than to grant blacks any measure of power across racial lines. These free blacks represented a threat to capital accumulation, a menace to slavery, and a challenge to the way of life that Baltimore County's prosperous white farmers and Baltimore city's mercantile entrepreneurs sought to enjoy. But still they were there, as difficult to eradicate as mosquitoes in the countryside or rats in the city, and no more desirable a presence than other vermin to many white citizens of Baltimore County.[23]

Seeing his slaves as victims of the free black Johnson, incapable of asserting their own will and lacking the initiative and capacity for setting their own course, was the only explanation that made any sense to Gorsuch. He saw the slaves as passive, complacent, incompetent, and incapable of making their own way in the world. He worried that they would starve to death. He reasoned that they had no good cause to run away and believed for a long time that they would come wandering back any day begging for the forgiveness which he, as a New Testament father, would bestow on the prodigal slaves. The fugitives, who were all between the ages of nineteen and twenty-two, were to be freed in a scant few years in any event. What exactly had they to fear from such a benevolent master as himself? Even as the days passed into weeks, months, and then a year without their return, Gorsuch continued to believe that his "boys" really wanted to come back, that if he could just talk to them, tell them he intended no punishment for the crime they had committed, they would return gladly to Retreat. On the other hand, Gorsuch wanted to see Johnson, the free black "instigator" of the robbery and escape, punished severely by the law.[24]

Gorsuch tried his best to locate Johnson and the four "boys" the free black had "led" away. First, Gorsuch sought and received an official requisition from the governor of Maryland to assist in the capture and extradition of Johnson from Pennsylvania. Then, when he thought that he knew where the slaves were living, he procured the same sort of document to buttress his legal right to bring them back home. When Gorsuch's son Dickinson traveled to Harrisburg with the legal papers, however, he found Pennsylvania officials with whom he discussed the case unsympathetic. Clearly, they were not going to help, and likely they were going to resist any efforts to recapture and extradite the black men.[25]

Despite such obstacles, Gorsuch persisted, never giving up hope that he could find his slaves and bring them back to Baltimore County. His motivations are not obvious. Gorsuch never really explained why he poured time, money, and eventually his own blood into the attempt to re-enslave these four men. At first, to be sure, he thought that the men would willingly come home if only he could talk to them himself. Perhaps he persisted in a paternalistic concern that the "boys" were in trouble and needed his help. An economic explanation does not entirely account for the master's behavior during the two years following the escape. Gorsuch, like his neighbors, had already calculated that on balance slavery was an economic drain on his farm. He had already promised the four men in question their freedom upon reaching the age of twenty-eight, so as the years passed without their return, the amount of labor to be extracted from them was becoming less and less valuable.[26]

Available evidence about Edward Gorsuch's personality points in another direction. It was a matter of pride, of "honor," for him to recapture his slaves. The slaves' desire to run away and their ability to escape his dominion were an embarrassment, perhaps a humiliation, to the Maryland slave owner. Gorsuch saw himself as personally diminished in the eyes of his neighbors, his family, and the rest of the slaves on his farm. He felt betrayed by the slaves who had left and threatened by, perhaps even vulnerable to, the slaves who remained.[27]

As Bertram Wyatt-Brown has observed, honor was perhaps the central motivating force behind the public actions of Southern white men during the antebellum era. Whether behavior was rational, "wise, or fraught with risks" was of little moment to men whose greater concern was "the necessity for valiant action." In Edward Gorsuch's mental world, "fellow whites—as well as blacks themselves—would have despised a squeamish slaveholder who was unable to make his will felt." His good name, and that of his family and ancestors, was at risk. Gorsuch, like other Southern men of his day, would sacrifice his wealth, and even his life, to salvage the honor lost by the escape of his slaves. If it was the "threat of honor lost, no less than slavery," that led the South toward secession and Civil War, it was the same concern that propelled Edward Gorsuch down the road to his personal destruction. It was because Gorsuch symbolized the region's lost honor on the issue of fugitive slaves, embodied the values that motivated other Southern white men, and died a martyr to the cause that his death would become a cause célèbre in the South.[28]

Still, Gorsuch grossly underestimated the potential for violence in the confrontation that he sought to provoke between himself and the four escaped slaves. He did not, at least initially, intend to martyr himself on a field of honor. Southern masters had a difficult time imagining that their slaves could ever do them harm. This was partly an assessment of slave personality, a vision of African-Americans in bondage as "tamed" by the institution of slavery. Such attitudes were also a function of the masters' general belief that slaves felt a familial attachment to the whites who ruled over them. In some cases, this was true. But the unlocked doors, remarked on by surprised foreign travelers in the South, and the free access that slaves had to the houses of their masters, day and night, belied the reality of slave violence, which the masters psychologically suppressed. As Edward Ayers discovered in his study of Southern violence, "although whites considered most blacks to be thieves and knew that some blacks had killed whites, [they] did not generally consider slaves violent people." It was Gorsuch's valuation of honor and his assumptions about the personalities of the black men he had once enslaved and their affection for him that lay behind this master's single-minded pursuit of the fugitives.[29]

It is no less difficult to recover the perspective of the slaves than of the master. We cannot really know how the men who stole the wheat and made their escape perceived enslavement on Gorsuch's farm, except to reason from their actions that slavery was a greater burden than the master believed. Hypothesizing again from what we can learn about the perspective of other slaves who shared similar experiences, it seems that a master's lenity or the promise of freedom at some future date was no guarantee of contentment among the enslaved. Indeed, according to

Frederick Douglass, who had both generous and harsh masters during his youth as a Maryland slave, the more solicitous a master was about their welfare, the more likely human chattel would be to seek out their freedom. "Beat and cuff your slave," Douglass advised,

> keep him hungry and spiritless, and he will follow the chain of his master like a dog; but, feed and clothe him well,—work with him moderately—surround him with physical comfort,—and dreams of freedom intrude. Give him a *bad* master, and he aspires to a *good* master; give him a good master, and he wishes to become his *own* master.

Even a walk in the country, along a stream, or in a forest or field was likely to inspire a thirst for freedom in the slave for whom hope, rather than despair, was the guiding light. Freedom requires an act of imagination followed by an act of will. A master who gives sustenance to his slave's imagination should, according to Douglass, expect flight rather than gratitude. "The thought that men are made for other and better uses than slavery," Douglass remembered, "thrives best under the gentle treatment of a kind master." Promise him liberty tomorrow, and he will crave it today. Such is human nature. Such is the psychology of the slave.[30]

At best, the attitude of the young male slave toward the kind master was one of ambivalence and distrust. Male slaves, no less than their masters, were products of cultures in which honor and shame defined identity, determined a sense of self-worth, and dictated assertive action when the will and the body were not crushed by the weight of oppression. It was power that complicated the honor-shame paradigm for slaves. It was circumstance that determined how, where, and when they gave vent to the pent-up emotions repressed in the face of "the boss."[31]

According to Wyatt-Brown, the slave had options that permitted honorable subservience to the master. Some slaves, of course, became socialized to subordination, accepting the circumstances that brought them their shame. Others, more assertive and with greater self-esteem, found that technical compliance with their masters' orders left room for the maintenance of honor in a slowed work pace, intentional misunderstandings and mistakes, or the willful loss and destruction of tools. Adopting the guise of Sambo—the dumb, smiling, foot-shuffling fool—represented a third alternative that denied the system of honor and substituted a mask of shamelessness. Whatever choice the slave adopted, however, he paid a psychic price that was recoverable only by direct confrontation with the master or running away. Each required a compromise with the system, with the master, and with himself. It was the slave of some sensitivity, what Douglass termed "imagination," who faced the greatest dilemma: how, in the words of Wyatt-Brown, "to maintain dignity in the face of shamelessness by masters and even by fellow slaves." Again, it was these sensitive slaves, precisely the sort that Douglass saw as the products of life under a "good" master, who might be expected to take flight. These were the slaves least able, in an emotional sense, to live with the shame of involuntary servitude.[32]

So, the perennial question, why did not more slaves run away? Frederick Douglass offered several observations on this point, which historians have supplemented with several more. In the first place, as Douglass mentioned in the passage previously quoted, many slaves were so psychologically battered, so full of despair, that they were incapable of seizing the initiative to strike out on their own. The message delivered by their masters, and by society at large, that they were incompetent, dependent, born and bred to a servile status was received and, at some level, believed by many slaves. As Douglass suggested, those who lived under the worst conditions were most likely to be seized by a sense of utter hopelessness that kept them from acting in their own behalf.

Then, too, there were the ties to friends and family that kept many or most slaves in the environs of their servitude. "It is my opinion," Douglass contended, "that thousands would escape from slavery who now remain there, but for the strong chords of affection that bind them to their families, relatives, and friends." Only one of the four men who ran away from the Gorsuch farm was married, and there is no indication that he had any children. The four young men were at an age when kinship responsibilities did not yet outweigh the desire to do the best they could for themselves.[33]

It would be a mistake to underestimate the danger involved in an escape attempt or the degree to which the violence of the slave system functioned to discourage challenges to the regime. As Eugene Genovese has noted, what is most remarkable about challenges to the antebellum slave system is not that there were so few but that in the face of such daunting odds there were so many slaves who risked their lives for liberty's sake. About a thousand African-Americans took the risk each year during the 1850s, even after the federal Fugitive Slave Law added another hurdle to their race for freedom. Gorsuch's slaves were four among the 279 who escaped from Maryland during the twelve months preceding June 30, 1850; this was the highest number of losses for any slave state.[34]

The runaways from Gorsuch's farm were typical in a number of ways that help us to comprehend the meaning of their actions. Like 80 percent of those who ran to freedom, Gorsuch's ex-slaves were males between the ages of sixteen and thirty-five. They also conformed to the normal practice of fleeing in a group and in response to a specific incident for which they feared retribution. Like so many others who made their way surreptitiously to the North, Buley, Ford, and the two Hammonds fled a comparatively kind master, a comparatively lenient form of enslavement, the upper rather than the lower South, and the country rather than the city.[35]

Compared to the great mass of those who stayed behind, these runaways were confident men who had gotten a whiff of freedom on a breeze from the North. Just as the others who struck out across the border, these four men probably underestimated the trouble that lay ahead and the limits of freedom for African-Americans in a Northern state. Still, that is not to say that had they known all that lay before them the fugitives would have taken another course. Freedom is certainly its own reward, whatever the tribulations of independence, but that is not something that they could have easily explained to the master whose pride they had injured by running away. It had been a long time since the Gorsuches braved an Atlantic crossing and challenged a wilderness to realize their personal liberty. Perhaps they had forgotten what it meant to be unfree.

Rumor had it that Ford, Buley, and the Hammonds were somewhere in southeastern Pennsylvania, perhaps living a distance apart in Berks, Chester, or Montgomery County. Over the next two years, Gorsuch pursued every rumor, seized every opportunity to try communicating with the fugitives, but had difficulty pinning down exactly where they were. Perhaps the ex-slaves moved around to avoid detection, possibly the network of anti-slavery activists was better organized than those who worked against them, but it took time and money to determine with certainty where the men lived. The federal Fugitive Slave Law of 1850 removed impediments thrown up by officials in Pennsylvania, but the master still had to find the slaves.

A letter from an informant in Gorsuch's employ dated Lancaster County, 28 August 1851, removed this major obstacle to bringing the fugitives home. "Respected friend," the letter began,

> I have the required information of four men that is within two miles of each other. Now, the best way is for you to come as a hunter, disguised, about two days ahead of your son and let him come by way of Philadelphia and get the deputy marshal, John Nagle I think is his name. Tell him the situation and he can get force of the right kind. It will take about twelve so that they can divide and take them all within half an hour. Now, if you can come on the 2nd or 3rd of September come on & I will meet you at the gap when you get there. Inquire for Benjamin

Clay's tavern. Let your son and the marshal get out [at?] Kinyer's *[sic]* hotel. Now, if you cannot come at the time spoken of, write very soon and let me know when you can. I wish you to come as soon as you possibly can.

Very respectfully thy friend
William M.P.

This was exactly what Gorsuch had been waiting for. He must have been thrilled. Immediately, he began to make plans for the journey, recruiting several friends and relatives for the trip north. We do not know what the master of Retreat Farm was thinking as he prepared to meet his slaves. Gorsuch's actions suggest that he no longer believed the fugitives really wanted to come home, that he no longer was confident he could convince them to return to his farm. Edward Gorsuch packed guns, and so did the rest of his party.[36]

[2]

Black Images In White Minds

RELATIONS BETWEEN PEOPLE OF DIFFERENT RACES had changed in the North during the century preceding the escape of Edward Gorsuch's slaves. The abolition of slavery was central to this process, and the influx of fugitive slaves put an additional strain on the tolerance of whites for the blacks who lived in their midst. By the time the runaways from Retreat Farm crossed the Susquehanna River in late 1849, Pennsylvania's gradual emancipation law of 1780 had completed its work.[1] In Lancaster County, there were 348 slaves in 1790, 178 a decade later, 55 in 1830, and 2 in 1840; the last one died only a few years before Ford, Buley, and the two Hammonds arrived. Even in 1790, free blacks outnumbered slaves in Lancaster's population 545 to 348, and African-Americans represented about 2.5 percent (1.5 percent free, 1 percent slaves) of the county's inhabitants. At its antebellum peak in 1850, the number of blacks reached 3,614 (about 3.7 percent of the county's population). From there the number of African-Americans in Lancaster declined to 3,459 (just under 3 percent of county residents) ten years later as fear heightened by the Fugitive Slave Law drove hundreds to emigrate farther north to Canada.[2]

Perhaps the four fugitives had not believed the self-interested portrait of Northern white bigotry and free black poverty drawn by their master. Possibly they were surprised, as European visitors were during the 1830s and 1840s, that the "prejudice of race" was at least as bad in the North as in the slave states. "The Negro is free," Alexis de Tocqueville observed,

> but he can share neither the rights, nor the pleasures, nor the labor, nor the afflictions, nor the tomb of him whose equal he has been declared to be; and he cannot meet him upon fair terms in life or in death.

"Singular is the degree of contempt and dislike in which the free blacks are held in all the free States of America," Frederick Marryat recorded in his diary; "is this not extraordinary in a land which professes universal liberty, equality, and the rights of man?"[3]

Tocqueville hypothesized a causal connection between African-American freedom and white bigotry. "In the South," he reasoned,

> the master is not afraid to raise his slave to his own standing, beause he knows that he can in a moment reduce him to the dust at pleasure. In the North the white no longer distinctly perceives the barrier that separates him from the degraded race, and he shuns the Negro with the more pertinacity since he fears lest they should some day be confounded together.[4]

There is some truth in Tocqueville's diagnosis of racial intolerance in the North, but he lacked the sort of longer-term historical context for his observations that shows local relations between the races in a different light. In the eighteenth century, before the American Revolution, before Pennsylvania's gradual emancipation law even began to take effect, and before the influx of fugitive slaves from the South, there existed an inveterate prejudice against people of African ancestry who lived in the colony. Changes in the attitudes of whites toward blacks were subtle and slow, and for one brief period at the end of the eighteenth century there was even the promise of some improvement. But over the long term, the trend was certainly not from good to bad, from tolerance to intolerance, from sufferance to disdain.

Pennsylvania's first colonial law mentioning its black population did not distinguish between those who were free and those who were slaves. To white legislators in the Quaker-dominated assembly, race transcended class or status in a way impossible for blacks to overcome. Special "Negro courts" heard all cases concerning African-American defendants beginning in 1700 and meted out punishments significantly harsher than those reserved for white criminals. Blacks—free and enslaved—were whipped rather than fined for property crimes. None could be a witness against whites in criminal cases, which meant that blacks were fair game for white rapists, thieves, and assassins.[5]

A special law of 1726 made a legal distinction between free blacks and slaves for the first time, but for the purpose of placing additional restrictions on the movements of "free" blacks. According to the new law's preamble, experience had shown whites that "free negroes are an idle, slothful people, and often burdensome to the neighborhood and afford ill examples to other negroes." Therefore, the act sought to limit the size of the free black population by imposing a £30 indemnity on masters who manumitted their slaves. What is more, any able-bodied free black who, in the opinion of a magistrate, misspent his time could be returned to bondage for as long as the jurist saw fit.

Such unique burdens on African-Americans have led one historian to conclude recently that "the legal treatment of *free* blacks in colonial Pennsylvania appears to have been as restrictive and discriminatory as in any other colony." And according to A. Leon Higginbotham, Jr., "in one significant respect Pennsylvania treated free blacks even more harshly than did any of the southern colonies." Standard legal doctrine dictated that the children of free women of any race were also free, but in colonial Pennsylvania the children of *all* free blacks or mulattoes and *all* blacks freed by their masters before reaching the age of twenty-one years in the case of women and twenty-four for men were to be bound into the service of a white master until they reached those ages.[6]

Children of mixed racial unions endured an even harsher fate. These children were bound to white masters until reaching the age of thirty-one years. Clearly, the children were being punished for the "sin" of their parents. As embodiments of the racial amalgamation most feared by whites, these children were a marginal people in between the two races, who were no doubt singled out for more forms of harassment than this one law reveals. In such legislative enactments the fears and prejudices of white legislators are visible, and some of the limits on freedom for people of African and mixed racial heritage are revealed.

Another student of the African-American experience concludes that "slavery in Pennsylvania was not unique in its mildness," contrary to the colony's reputation among historians for racial liberalism. Merle G. Brouwer notes the harshness of punishments based on race and the prejudices of even the best white friends of black Pennsylvanians as evidence supporting this conclusion. A free black convicted of fornicating with a white was, according to law, sold into servitude for seven years, while the guilty white faced a maximum sentence of one year in prison and a fine of £50. Until a new law of 1706, black men condemned for attempted rape of white women were to be castrated; death was the punishment for blacks convicted of raping a white woman. A white man found guilty of raping a white woman was subject to a maximum of thirty-one lashes plus seven years in jail, and according to Brouwer, the punishment of white men was considerably more lenient than the law allowed.[7]

Beyond the laws, a few surviving court cases, and the comments of some comparatively liberal white men, we know little about the daily lives of African-Americans during the eighteenth century.[8] We do know that whites feared blacks and believed them capable of terrible violence—that is clear from the highly restrictive laws intended to limit their numbers and control those already in Pennsylvania. The records reveal few instances of blacks attacking Lancaster County whites over the course of the century.[9]

We can safely conclude that blacks despised their status as slaves, if only because so many malingered, broke tools, ran away, or even killed themselves to escape the service of their masters. We can be sure that Pennsylvania's African-Americans coveted their freedom, whether it came by flight, manumission, self-purchase, or after 1780 by the slow-working liberty of the state's gradual abolition law. Over 250 slaves fled from rural southeastern Pennsylvania between 1730 and 1755 alone, and only about fifty-three of them were ever caught. That tells us something about the attitude of Lancaster's slaves toward their status; it reveals something about their courage and their ingenuity in getting away.[10]

We cannot know how extraordinary was the experience of a slave who escaped in 1761 despite the iron collar around his neck, the handcuffs on his wrists, and the six-foot chain that encumbered him further. We can only imagine with horror what it must have been like for a free black to be imprisoned on suspicion of being a slave, to languish in jail while advertisements were placed to see if any master came forward to claim his "property," and if no "master" showed up, to be sold into bondage, nonetheless, until the "free" black worked off the costs of his incarceration. The humiliation, anger, fear, and despair that must have swept over black Pennsylvanians in waves is pretty much lost to us, even though we try, and inevitably fail, to picture ourselves in the same place.[11]

Imagine the experience of James Daniel, a free black man who had fought in the American Revolution under General Nathaniel Greene. In 1782, Daniel was impoverished after he got out of the army, so he indentured himself to a Lancaster County farmer. The farmer, in turn, kidnapped Daniel, transported him across the Maryland line, and sold him into slavery. Daniel escaped, ran North, and arrived at the office of the Pennsylvania Abolition Society with his "master" in hot pursuit. Daniel was eventually set free, but after a harrowing ordeal. We can only guess how many similar incidents from Lancaster County and elsewhere in the state did not turn out so well.[12]

Some historians believe that in the first half of the eighteenth century the ownership of slaves in Pennsylvania was more a means to display one's wealth than to become richer still. As house servants, liverymen, and carriage drivers, slaves became one among other affectations of style for an emerging provincial elite. According to Alan Tully, "it was the rich who, along with the silver watch, the showy pacing horse and the expensive personal wardrobe, acquired the Negro slave," at least up until the late 1750s. The initial outlay of cash to purchase a slave (£45 Pennsylvania currency) exceeded the total personal estate of over one-third of the region's taxable residents and added to the yearly tax assessment of the owner. The law also required that, at the time of manumission, masters post a substantial bond (£30) against the possibility that a freed black would become a burden on the community. So the ownership of slaves was beyond the means of most white Lancastrians up to the middle of the century and was not perceived as economically desirable before that time.[13]

After 1758, and into the 1760s, labor shortages brought an increase in local purchases of slaves, which were often financed by loans, to the point where more than one in every six southeastern Pennsylvania households was involved in slaveholding. But still, most masters never owned more than one slave, usually a field hand or a household servant, less frequently a craftsman's assistant or an innkeeper's maid. Over time, most African-Americans in rural southeastern Pennsylvania worked on farms. Slaves, and then free blacks, were also significant in the early years of the region's iron industry; and after emancipation, as before, they continued to work in some trades, particularly leather and building, and as house servants.[14]

For Lancaster County, the eighteenth-century record is thinner than for Philadelphia and for Pennsylvania at large; but there is no reason to believe that slaveholders were any more lenient or racial prejudice any less virulent in this rural county than throughout the colony and then Commonwealth. Race rather than status or class fixed the quality of life for Lancaster's black residents. African-Americans were segregated in church services and cemeteries, and even Quakers isolated blacks in their Meetings. John Woolman, the New Jersey Quaker and anti-slavery reformer, thought of African-Americans as "far from being our kinsfolk" and "of a vile stock." Benjamin Franklin, who was not a Quaker and did own slaves though president of Pennsylvania's reconstituted anti-slavery society in the 1780s, believed the majority of blacks were "of a plotting disposition, dark, sullen, malicious, revengeful and cruel in the highest degree." And these were two of the best white friends that black people had in the Delaware Valley during the eighteenth century.[15]

There were, to be sure, instances of humanity by white Pennsylvanians to black ones during the colonial period, but historians Brouwer and Higginbotham believe that those were the exceptions, even among Quakers and other more racially tolerant whites. The likes of such white men as Anthony Benezet, the Quaker reformer and educator of African-American children, were not the rule. Brouwer finds no evidence that Quaker slave owners were "particularly noted for leniency," even though "humane exceptions can be found in every age and every place where slavery has been practiced." [16]

As Pennsylvania Quakers came, by stages, to see the light on the issue of slavery, they ceased to engage personally in the buying and selling of slaves, manumitted their own chattel laborers, and a number of them worked to meliorate the condition of free blacks. Some—apparently most—bestowed a freedom settlement on ex-slaves, which they calculated by subtracting the costs of purchase and sustenance from an estimated value of labor over the period of enslavement. And it was not unusual for blacks in southeastern Pennsylvania to continue working on a salaried basis for their ex-masters, with whom they enjoyed amicable relations. Even after 1776, however, when the Philadelphia Yearly Meeting reached the conclusion that one could not be both a member of the Meeting and an owner of slaves, some Quakers resisted such enlightened goals. Noah Dixon told a visitation committee from the Uwchlan Monthly Meeting in 1777 that, in his opinion, slavery "is a good thing. It keeps them apart so they will not do misdeeds." The 1797 edition of the Society's *Rules of Discipline* reminded members that they must release all their slaves and that their charitable responsibilities toward blacks did not end upon manumission. The 1806 version pointed out that hiring slave labor was also inconsistent with the Society's testimony against trafficking in slaves. [17]

The limits of empathy across racial lines, even among this socially enlightened religious group, were quite clear. Just as in Baltimore County, where the Quaker miller betrayed Gorsuch's slaves to their master, Pennsylvania's Quakers would go only so far—individually and collectively—in their relationships with blacks. African-Americans were more or less welcome to attend Quaker Meetings, as long as they sat in special sections reserved for members of their race. Full membership in the Society of Friends was another matter, however, and that is where Meetings generally drew the line on their brotherly feelings for blacks. [18]

Throughout the antebellum period, Quakers testified publicly and privately against slavery and in behalf of the interests of free blacks. Over time, however, the Society became re-absorbed in its own internal problems and resisted any affiliation with the radical abolitionist movement, leaving the fight against racial injustice primarily in the hands of individual members. And the prejudice against African-Americans, which the Quakers shared in kind if not in degree with other whites, grew rather than abated over time.

John Chandler, a British Friend traveling through Pennsylvania in the early 1840s, was among those who commented on the racism of Quakers he met. Chandler believed that Philadelphia, the City of Brotherly Love, merited the name "more in its origin, when it rose fresh from the wilderness, than it does now." It was not just the working-class whites, according to Chandler, but also the better educated who harbored a "great dislike to their Coloured fellow-citizens":

> The members of our religious society form a numerous body in the city, and many of them are wealthy, and have proportionate influence; but the general prejudice of the community on this head is too deeply rooted for them, individually or unitedly to overcome. In fact, they make no effort to overcome it. . . . They are kind to the coloured people: they relieve their necessities; they visit their sick; they educate their orphan children, and perform to them many disinterested acts of love and mercy; but still they seem to consider them as aliens—as a people who have no right to a possession in the land that gave them birth.[19]

The limited sufferance described by Chandler was the best that any African-American could expect from a white person in Pennsylvania; and the worst was much worse, indeed. Blacks would have to rely on themselves, supplemented by aid from the few whites who bore them goodwill as the nineteenth century began. African-American institutions—churches, schools, clubs, and self-protection associations—would have to pick up where white philanthropy and the protection of the laws left off. We do know that prior to 1817 whites permitted Lancaster's African-Americans to worship in St. James Episcopal and Trinity Lutheran churches. As late as 1820, blacks could still be buried in special sections of the county's "white" cemeteries, although the practice was controversial by that time.[20]

The possibility, and the limitations, of such amicable integration across racial lines is suggested by the earliest graphic depiction of an African-American from this region of rural Pennsylvania (Figure 2.1). Local artist Lewis Miller drew on a childhood memory for the scene inside York's Lutheran Church on a Sunday morning in 1800. Among the hundreds of congregants shown in the picture, in the corner farthest removed from the central focus of attention is a lone black man huddled in humble supplication. Whites are passing him on the stairs as they climb to the balcony; he is apparently all but invisible to them and others gathered for the worship service.

The posture, location, and lone presence of the black man in Miller's painting are revealing. There is literally no room for even this one

FIGURE 2.1. Lewis Miller, "In Side of the Old Lutheran Church in 1800, York, Pa." *(with permission of the Historical Society of York County)*

African-American in the crowded pews of the church. What would happen if several more African-Americans sought even such marginal inclusion as that claimed by the solitary figure on the back stairs? They would be noticed; they would be in the way; it would become clearer that they did not belong.

Over time, growth of the African-American population, fueled in part by an influx of Southern blacks—both fugitives and recently manumitted slaves—tested even this limited tolerance of whites for people who were racially and culturally different. The interracial accommodation of eighteenth-century Lancaster, which was based on the total subordination of blacks, crumbled under the stresses of change. As historian Winthrop D. Jordan noticed on the national scene:

> Whatever their behavior . . . free Negroes constituted a threat to white society which . . . arose within the white man as a less than conscious feeling that a people who had always been absolutely subjected were now in many instances outside the range of the white man's unfettered power.[21]

Violence involving African-Americans increased over time in response to such bigotry and to social upheaval, which included growth of the black population, the threat to white identity posed by economically successful African-Americans, and the impoverished conditions in which a growing number of blacks continued to live.

The fugitives from Gorsuch's farm, as others before and around them, found that white Lancastrians had a limited range of images to which they expected blacks to conform; what they could not know is how such depictions had changed over time. Some assumptions about the character and capacities of African-Americans came from personal acquaintance with blacks, but even then cultural stereotypes filtered information about who a black person was, or could be. Jordan suggests that "in all societies men tend to extrapolate from social status to actual inherent character, to impute to individuals characteristics suited to their social roles."[22]

During the late eighteenth century, there were several black personae that supplement those in Lewis Miller's painting. Lancaster's newspapers provided readers with portrayals of African-Americans drawn from local, regional, national, and international sources. In part, these were selected by editors from a wider array of stories involving African-Americans. Advertisements for runaway slaves also included behavioral descriptions that reflected cultural stereotyping. Both news stories and advertisements for fugitives were generally, but not always, drafted by writers who lived outside the county and then reprinted in local newspapers.

For the purposes of this chapter, the question is not so much whether the likenesses were "true," although it would be interesting to know how "facts" were transformed—selected, interpreted, and perhaps even re-cast—in the hands of writers and editors for a variety of ends and in light of their own assumptions about African-American character. Of more significance here is the cumulative sense in which readers were exposed to a fairly narrow range of African, African-Caribbean, and African-American images, and how those narrowed, sharpened, and changed over time.[23] Such portrayals give us clues about the attitudes toward blacks in the white community and also to the ways that information from outside the region contributed to changing local impressions of African-Americans.

All of the negative qualities assigned to blacks during the eighteenth century continued to appear in the Lancaster press through the Civil War, although images of African-American violence and stealth became more frequent. The most generous portrayals of the mental capacities of blacks—and here opinion was divided between biological determinists and environmentalists—were often transformed into hostile depictions of African-Americans' talent for outwitting naive and trusting whites. To simplify the process only a bit, the image of the loyal and sometimes brave black servant—who was always outnumbered in white minds by African-American cowards, drunkards, fools, thieves, and murderers—was replaced over time by two all-encompassing types: the black victim and the black perpetrator of violence. The guise of the faithful domestic came to be seen as a disguise. Even many of those writers and editors who continued to speak out for the abolition of slavery, for the rights of blacks, and against the worst abuses of Northern bigotry, believed African-Americans to be alien beings who ought to return to Africa.[24]

There were, of course, unsavory white characters in the newspapers as well. Neither editors nor readers were so bigoted or so blind as to believe that African-Americans monopolized all of humanity's vices. White murderers, thieves, drunkards, and fools also appeared in the press. But the disproportionate share of negative images were of blacks, in a region where they constituted a tiny fraction of the populace. And more important, the few positive depictions of African-Americans in Lancaster's newspapers (and even fewer over time) were eclipsed by a significantly wider cast of white characters, many or most of them admirable for the very qualities that the blacks seemed to lack. For every Toussaint L'Ouverture—"a truly great man. . . . [of] sound judgement, a penetrating mind, a correct observation, great industry, and unbounded energy"—

and there was only *one* from the late eighteenth century through the Civil War, there were scores of white statesmen, philanthropists, reformers, men of science, medicine, letters, and law presented as models of their race. For every loyal and faithful African-American servant or slave in the news, and there were a few before the second decade of the nineteenth century, there were dozens of black robbers and assassins; Lancaster's newspaper editors found very little to admire about black people during the thirty years after 1830.[25]

The earliest surviving images of African-Americans in Lancaster's newspapers from the 1790s often came in advertisements for escaped slaves, which presented them as foolish or "simple," incompetent, sneaky—"a very artful fellow"—impudent—"very impertinent, and a great liar"—evil—"an arch villain and very cowardly"—and prone to excessive drinking—"very quarrelsome when in liquor." Masters sometimes described African-American fugitives by their behavior in the company of whites—"he has when spoken to a very simple look with his eyes" or a "down look" or is "very apt to laugh" or is "embarrassed when spoken to."[26]

Masters often remembered their escaped slaves as thieves and otherwise dishonest, and there were numerous stories in the press that supplemented this image, reinforcing the stereotype and giving it texture and hue. The emphasis in reports of robberies by blacks was more on the violence perpetrated by African-American thieves than on the financial losses sustained. The stock images were of random violence, unsuspecting travelers waylaid on the road, or innocent white families who had the locked doors to their homes battered down by wild-eyed blacks. There were stories about African-American strangers beating householders senseless and abusing horrified wives who came to their husbands' defense, all for a pittance of cash and goods that the victims would have surrendered peacefully if given the chance. The *Lancaster Journal* also carried stories about African-American mail robbers, the attempted murder and hold-up of a toll keeper on the Lancaster highway by two black men, and dozens of anecdotes about small but frequent pilfering by black servants and slaves from as far away as Louisiana and New York.[27]

More often, murder rather than plunder seemed the sole goal of the African-Americans depicted in the press. Arson, poisoning, and slave insurrections were news staples from the late eighteenth century through the Civil War. A frequent theme highlighted in such stories during the late eighteenth and early nineteenth centuries was that of betrayal by servants and slaves who were ill-treated by whites. The *Lancaster Journal* printed in full, for example, the confession of "Negro Chloe," condemned to death in nearby Carlisle for murdering two daughters in the white family she served. "The reason I killed them," her white amanuensis recorded,

> was not because I had any spite or malice against them; on the contrary, I loved them both. My motive in the first place was this; I knew that the children were compelled by my mistress to give information respecting some parts of my conduct; for which I was severely corrected, far beyond the demerit of the fault. To cut off this means of information was the first end I promised myself; but my second and greatest motive was, to bring all the misery I possibly could upon the family, and particularly upon my mistress.

In a backhanded way, this "confession" was an anti-slavery appeal and a plea for greater kindness, fairness, and sympathy for blacks. As such, it was the product of a time and place wherein people saw slavery as evil but harbored more fear than affection for African-Americans. The image projected by the rest of the story, in which the murders were recounted in horrible detail, was one of an unbounded capacity for violence harbored in the breast of even the seemingly meekest and most loyal of family servants.[28]

Most of the murders by blacks described in the press were similar to Chloe's in the sense that they were committed by slaves against members of the white families they served. Slave insurrections throughout the South and the Caribbean were, of course, common fare and were reported in Lancaster's newspapers in livid detail. Women were more often the victims than men in the cases of individual murders, and when the perpetrators in such cases were black men, editors played the imagery of threatened white womanhood to the hilt. "HORRID!" was the screaming headline, and unrequited lust was the motive, in a story about the attempted rape and murder of a New York woman by a sixteen-year-old slave on her farm. According to the *Journal*, revenge against a Kentucky master led to the brutal murder of his daughter by a slave. African-American women were also quite capable of violence, as Lancaster readers learned not only from Chloe's "confession." The *Journal* reported that two female field slaves murdered their mistress, whose corpse was later chopped into at least eight pieces and floated down the James River. More often, female slaves—and male cooks as well—used poison as the chosen instrument of death; but since dosage was critical—too much could be tasted or induce immediate vomiting, too little would bring on painful symptoms, but nothing more—the poisoners written up in the newspapers almost always failed. Occasionally, a slave harbored the mistaken belief that if she could wipe out the whole white family at one meal, there would be nobody left to own her, and she would be free. More often, revenge for a particular injustice was apparently the goal, although accumulated rage was sometimes enough to trigger a mass-murder attempt.[29]

The numerous failed poisonings also reflected another characteristic of African-Americans as portrayed in the press. In addition to being violent, blacks also seemed thoughtless and inept to reporters, editors, and no doubt readers as well. Sometimes the "incompetence" of blacks saved whites from the most violent intentions of the African-Americans around them, but it could also result in occasionally fatal accidents. The *Journal* reported, for example, that a slave girl accidentally swallowed about thirty sewing pins, from which she died slowly and in excruciating pain. There were a number of stories over the course of sixty years about black children injuring themselves or accidentally killing others while playing with guns, and not one about similar accidents among whites. Given the expected incidence of such calamities in a gun-toting society and the newspapers' interest in violence from across the continent and around the world, the race specificity of these stories must have been a matter of selection by the editors rather than a mere reflection of available news. And accounts of African-American servants clumsily breaking household items (which we should suspect were often not accidents), losing control of horse-drawn carriages because of inattention, drowning or catching themselves on fire—despite numerous warnings to take better care—were much more frequent than similar stories about whites.

There are no doubt a number of mutually reinforcing explanations for the focus on mishaps involving African-Americans in a population that was preponderantly white. It is possible that such events did involve blacks out of proportion to their numbers in the population. We should not be surprised if African-Americans bore a disproportionate share of the dirtiest, most dangerous, and least desirable work; or that their judgment, balance, and skill were more often affected by dietary deficiencies, physical debilities, consumption of alcohol, and lack of sleep. Surely, as historians of slavery tell us, many "accidents" by slaves, including some in which blacks incapacitated themselves, were willful acts of destruction that reflected either an attempt to avoid work or to "punish" the master in ways that were comparatively safe. Beyond such possible explanations, it is still striking that newspaper editors found so few comparable stories about whites or deemed them less newsworthy. At least in part, the explanation must include the stereotypical roles assigned to blacks by this culture and the purposes for which the stories were intended. Reports of self-destruction by blacks were clearly presented as moral tales, and were perhaps even read aloud by the master of the household as injunctions to his careless servants.[30]

The slant of such stories is often revealing, as in the case of the slave girl who caught her clothes on fire when she reached for something on the mantlepiece. According to the account reprinted in the *Lancaster Intelligencer*, when the young woman, whose clothes were ablaze, ran for help, the fire spread from the slave to her mistress's curtains. The white woman's immediate reaction was to extinguish the flames on her furnishings, by which time the slave was beyond help. The mistress's priorities provoked no comment by the reporter or the editor who reprinted the account from a Norfolk newspaper, and the moral of the story was clear from the title—"An Awful Admonition to Careless Servants."[31]

Lancaster's newspapers reprinted numerous such stories about the inadvertent destruction of property by blacks; but arson and interpersonal violence were often undeniably intentional and of even more interest to Lancastrians. Though stories about accidental self-destruction were more common, the papers also reported spectacular suicides by blacks much more frequently than similar stories about whites. The *Journal*, for example, reported that a black woman threw her children and then herself down a well; and that a slave in nearby York, Pennsylvania, hanged both her infant and herself.[32]

The few African-American characteristics presented in a positive light during the late eighteenth century included musical skills—"inclined to play on the fiddle"—deference, strength, and good health—"bidable, strong and healthy." Most of all, whites seemed to respect those African-Americans whose loyalty included the willingness to sacrifice their own lives to save their masters. Stories about a black servant rushing back into a burning house to attempt a bold rescue and about a slave who threw himself between his master and *white* assassins were the most striking examples of this type.[33]

Then, in the early nineteenth century, things changed in the selection and reprinting of stories about African-Americans. Negative characteristics gained even greater precedence—in frequency and kind—over any positive portrayals of blacks, and the perception of the African-American capacity for loyalty almost disappeared from the newspapers. In the era of slave revolts, in Haiti and the Southern United States, stories about black arsonists entirely supplanted those describing heroic acts by loyal African-American servants. There was greater consistency in the negative images of blacks over time. Anecdotes, news stories, and advertisements continued to project images of carelessness, incompetence, foolishness, thievery, and stealth, but these were supplemented, and in some senses transformed, by portrayals of blacks as shrewd, calculating, and evil. Numerous stories of attempts to poison white families suggested that African-Americans' apparent affection for the white children they raised was only a ruse.

Although many of the portraits of violence by blacks came from outside the region, their selection by editors for republication in Lancaster's newspapers reflected not just changes in the available news but also growing local fears as the county's free black population increased. The York arson conspiracy of 1803 appeared to Lancaster's residents as a local symptom of the wider problem of African-American violence that they read about in stories from as far away as New Hampshire, South Carolina, and the West Indies.[34] Over a period of three weeks during February and March, six fires of suspicious origin occurred in the town without any suspects coming to light. Then, according to the local press, a black girl misunderstood her instructions, tried to burn down a barn at noon rather than midnight, and was caught in the act. Based on her (no doubt coerced) confession, townsmen arrested twenty-one African-Americans and several whites suspected of participating in the arson ring; eventually six blacks went to prison for the crimes.

The *York Recorder* was the main source of public information about the fires, which it diagnosed as a consequence of anger among the town's blacks over the conviction of an African-American woman for trying to poison two whites. In a search for systemic causes of the conflagration, the court also noted that the borough was "infested with some disorderly houses," which served as rendezvous for enslaved and free blacks. Besides closing down such illicit gathering places, magistrates would try to keep better track of black residents—who they were, where they lived, and whether they belonged. Basically, the problem appeared to be one of control, of bringing order to a disorderly population of vagrants and outsiders whose cheap labor was useful but whose presence constituted a threat to the safety of the community.[35]

Violence perpetrated by African-Americans seemed an increasing threat. Only a short time before—during the brief thaw in race relations that accompanied the American Revolution and brought about the state's gradual emancipation law—newspapers had portrayed some blacks as passive sufferers of brutality. But now again, as during the colonial period, African-Americans appeared quite frightening to whites. The pictures in Lewis Miller's sketchbook reflect such changes, as the prayerful supplicant (Figure 2.1) is replaced over time by gun-toting, fist-fighting blacks (Figures 2.2 and 2.3). How much of the changing depiction of African-Americans in the newspapers and paintings was a matter of white percep-

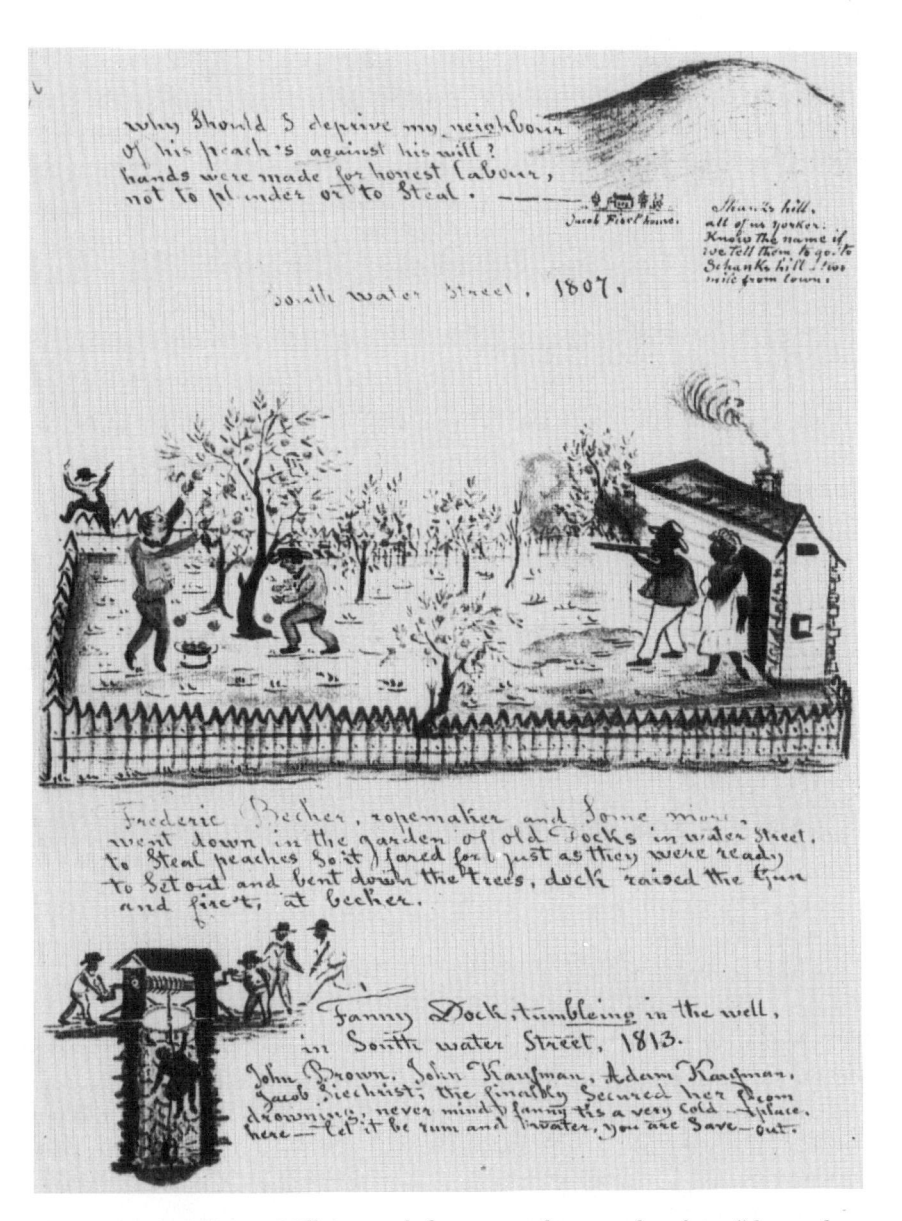

FIGURE 2.2. Lewis Miller, untitled, men stealing peaches from "the garden of old Docks," and "Fanny Dock tumbleing [*sic*] in the well" (*with permission of the Historical Society of York County*)

FIGURE 2.3. Lewis Miller, "A Fight on the Common" (*with permission of the Historical Society of York County*)

tions, and how much was real is impossible to say. We cannot know, for example, whether justice was done in the York arson case, whether the conspiracy was simply a figment of white fears and a coerced confession from a frightened young girl. But the flames and the linkage of local blacks to a conspiracy to burn down the town provide some indication of the suspicions—and perhaps the violent reality—that affected race relations early in the nineteenth century, as more African-Americans became free, more free blacks moved into the region, and news of violence by peoples of African heritage in other places was reported more frequently and in greater detail.[36]

Lancaster city's black population was increasing at a rate three times greater than that of the white between 1790 and 1810—126 percent compared to 43 percent—a trend that continued into the 1820s. To some whites, at least, it seemed like a flood and was about as welcome as a deluge. The growth was from a very small base; by 1820, after an increase of another 42 percent in the black population, there were still only 308 African-Americans among the 6,633 residents of the town—less than 5 percent—but whites noticed the change.

Beginning in the 1820s, white citizens from Lancaster and Pennsylvania's other southern counties continually petitioned the state legislature to stop the immigration of blacks from the South. Bills to this end did not receive the support of both houses in the same year, but in 1829 state lawmakers did agree to a statement that removal of African-Americans would be "highly auspicious to the best interests of the country," and they endorsed the efforts of the American Colonization Society to bring that about. There were other testaments to increasing fear and hostility toward blacks. The revised state constitution of 1837 limited voting to whites and was the specific outcome of a Bucks County election in which African-American ballots were believed decisive in a closely contested poll. Again, as long as there was only a meaningless handful of black voters, their presence could be tolerated, indeed pointed to with pride as symbols of the community's liberality; but when the numbers of black freeholders rose, made a difference, put African-Americans in a position even to make demands for fair treatment, then they became a threat that whites wanted quashed.[37]

It was during the 1820s and 1830s in Lancaster, as throughout the North, that the increased presence of blacks led whites to try to make them less visible, less threatening, and less part of "their" world. While once everyone had understood the rules of racial segregation, and whereas the presence of a small number of inconspicuous blacks could be tolerated because it went almost unnoticed, now whites found a need for even greater control, and the price was further restrictions on the lives of "free" blacks. In Lancaster city, it was fire and fear accompanied by the increased numbers of African-Americans that led to greater vigilance. In January 1820, the *Intelligencer* reported the devastation of Savannah, Georgia, by fire. Two months later, the *Journal* suggested a connection between the Savannah conflagration, a rash of local fires of suspicious origin, and the formation of two fire companies in Lancaster.[38]

The next step, as in York seventeen years earlier, was to begin more systematic surveillance of the black population. A city ordinance adopted in May 1820 required all "free persons of color" to register with the mayor. One consequence was creation of the "Negro Entry Book," which local historian Leroy Hopkins has transcribed and published. The 340 entries constitute an African-American city directory for the years from 1820 to 1849 and provide a wealth of information that otherwise would be lost to us. The entry book reveals that there was no concentration of blacks into ghettos during this period and that ownership of homes by them was rare. The unsurprising evidence that African-Americans generally occupied the lowest rung of the city's economic ladder is supplemented by information about the skilled and semiskilled black middle class. Beginning, as it does, at a moment of profound change in local race relations, the entry book also helps us to chart that process.[39]

The entry on James Clendenin, for example, tells us something about the emergence of propertied black leaders in this local setting and helps us put faces on the statistics about economic change. The Lancaster tax list for 1797 identified Clendenin as the first black property owner in the borough and as a painter by profession. By 1800, he was no longer paying any ground rent, which meant that he owned his house and land outright. The assessment valued Clendenin's property at two hundred dollars. By 1820, he had become more prosperous still. According to the registry book:

BLOODY DAWN

> James Clendenin, a mulatto enters that he is about sixty-five years of
> age, resides in Mussertown in the City of Lancaster, is a householder,
> by occupation a painter and glazier, has a wife named Elizabeth but no
> children, has a bound mulatto boy named William Clendenin about 10
> years of age, learning said trades, and a mulatto girl about seven years
> of age, named Hannah Clark.[40]

This kind of moderate economic success brought new standing to some
members of the black community during the early nineteenth century. It
also exacerbated white fears of amalgamation and made working-class whites
jealous of African-American economic achievements, which heightened
interracial violence (see Chapter 9). Throughout the antebellum North,
according to Leon Litwack, the economic achievement of blacks brought
down upon them "even greater hostility and suspicion" from whites:

> Northern whites had come to accept irresponsibility, ignorance, and
> submissiveness as peculiar Negro characteristics, as natural products of
> the Negroes' racial inferiority. Consequently, those who rose above de-
> pravity failed to fit the stereotype and somehow seemed abnormal, even
> menacing.[41]

Although whites believed that black transients had to be watched and
better controlled—that "troublemakers" who stole, started fires, and
threatened the peace of the city generally came from outside the area—
many also feared the likes of James Clendenin for what he was and for
what he symbolized about the possibilities for African-Americans to challenge and break the stereotypical roles in which they were cast. One or
two propertied blacks could be tolerated, just as the lone black on the
back stairs in Lewis Miller's painting could be suffered to stay. But a
rising black middle class was a different matter and, as we shall see in
Chapters 8 and 9, became the focus of violence in Lancaster County more
than once.

These middle-class blacks were a socially critical group, instrumental
in the formation of African-American churches and, with the sufferance
and assistance of whites, in the establishment of the local anti-slavery
society. Historian Carl Oblinger found that only the wealthiest of these
blacks had "recent, observable contact with the white Quaker abolitionists"; so such men as James Clendenin, Stephen Smith, and William
Whipper were interracial mediators, in addition to their other roles. And
it was the African-American chimney sweeps, skilled and semiskilled ar-

tisans, and barbers in Lancaster and Columbia boroughs who, in concert with other black property owners, helped in shadowy and now mostly lost ways to assist fugitives from slavery.[42]

Middle-class blacks were also different from the fugitives in a number of ways. Nearly all of them were mulattoes—less black—than those who arrived in Lancaster County hungry and scared. Over 80 percent descended from families that had lived in the region for more than one generation, while fewer than 10 percent of the laboring-class blacks had resided in the county for more than twenty years. Since only one-eighth of all blacks worked as skilled or nonmanual laborers in 1850, and only one-tenth could say the same in 1860, this was truly an elite, and one whose numbers were in decline at the time of the Christiana Riot. Along with the fugitives and the other local free blacks, African-Americans of property and standing also were scared—frightened of their white neighbors (and probably of the black laboring classes as well), of slave catchers to whom one kidnapped black was worth as much as another, and of the new Fugitive Slave Law. It was an era of change, some of it good, but most of it bad; and wealth provided little insulation from injustice, violence, and death. As a consequence, the most successful of Lancaster's blacks moved away in the 1850s, leaving even fewer philanthropic resources to assist a growing indigent population.[43]

The rest of the black community was even more exposed to the rough knocks of the marketplace, the bigotry of whites, and the shortcomings of justice under the law from the 1830s onward. The consequences included severe economic instability for working-class blacks. Day-laboring jobs left them unemployed for at least a hundred days a year. Class stratification accelerated within the black community; there was a visible and growing gap between the 5 percent at the top and the 70 percent that fell into what Oblinger terms the working- and under-classes during the 1840s. An increasingly large pool of itinerant workers traversed the area, evoking racial hostility and committing petty property crimes. Although African-Americans represented only $\frac{1}{34}$ of Pennsylvania's population, they made up one-third of the prisoners in the state's jails. During the 1840s and 1850s, Irish workers were competing successfully for jobs as carters and porters, which were once the sole province of blacks. Economic hard times in the late 1840s resulted in even greater hostility between Irish and black laborers and an increase in work-related violence. In 1842, Irish coal miners battled with African-Americans who competed for their jobs; in 1853, armed blacks replaced striking Irish railroad workers. According to Oblinger, between 1800 and 1860, at least a fourth of the black population . . . fell into poverty and disappeared either through death or transiency. This downward pressure on the black population increased towards mid-century, and only eased in the 1860's. The black poor were in a desperate condition. Ignored by the community, particularly after the mid-1820s, their death rates skyrocketed. The main community effort was directed at their removal either through fugitive aid or indentureships with farmers.[44]

Between 1830 and 1860 over five thousand African-Americans arrived in the region; about 20 percent of these fugitives and freed blacks from the South died within five years after securing their freedom. The death rate for impoverished blacks in southeastern Pennsylvania was better than a hundred out of a thousand, compared to forty-five per thousand for indigent whites. During the 1850s, increasing numbers of black children were growing up on the streets of Lancaster's towns, unsupervised by parents and often drawn to juvenile gangs that were responsible for much of the region's petty crime. This was the nature of freedom for fugitives who crossed the Mason-Dixon Line at about the same time as the four men from Edward Gorsuch's farm.[45]

Life for those blacks who were born in the region was also getting worse. During the 1840s and 1850s, people of African descent were losing the skilled work that members of their community had held for generations. Many were thrown out of their jobs and saw their sons denied apprenticeships in their trades.[46] Such changes were part of transformations in the craft system that were unsettling for white artisans as well as for black; they were also partly a consequence of competition from immigrant groups in trades that had once been monopolized by African-Americans.[47] But the story is much more complicated than that.

The changes that began earlier in the century and became increasingly visible from the 1820s to the 1850s were more than reflexive responses to an expanding market economy. They were also a product of white reactions to the increasing numbers of African-Americans in the region and of a diminishing tolerance for the presence of blacks. The unsavory images of African-Americans predated these changes, as local newspapers reveal, and were only enhanced by the arrival of so many poor, ignorant, and culturally alien fugitives during the antebellum decades. At the same time, there was a backlash—local and national—against the perceived social and political threats from radical abolitionism beginning in the 1820s, which occurred in the context of new "scientific" theories of racial inferiority.

In the nation at large, the persuasive powers of environmentalist philosophy—the belief that racial groups were products of their surroundings and that blacks would become more like whites in America over time— began to erode during the second decade of the nineteenth century. By the 1830s there was a wide-ranging debate between environmentalists and biological determinists, which by the 1840s and 1850s was, for the most part, resolved in favor of biology. According to historian George M. Fredrickson, the biological school "saw the Negro as a pathetically inept creature who was a slave to his emotions, incapable of progressive development and self-government because he lacked the white man's enterprise and intellect." In 1838, a writer for the *Lancaster Intelligencer* contributed a series of essays intended to demonstrate that blacks were unalterably inferior to whites. "Climate and its consequences," he asserted, "may effect them exteriorly, but it never can operate to change them to a different species of mankind. . . . It is well known that Africans, in their own country, left to their own unaided exertions, have not, in a long course of ages, made one single step in intelligence, industry or enterprize; one single progressive movement in refinement or any of the arts that render society agreeable, or life a blessing." The thrust of his argument, according to "Vindex," was not hostile toward African-Americans, just realistic:

> In attempting to show the mental inferiority of the negro to the white or Caucasian race, it is not my intention to make the fact an excuse for oppression or injustice towards them; but simply to make use of it to show the utter impracticability of Abolitionists elevating them to an equality with the whites. They are not only mentally but physically incapable of enjoying such privileges.[48]

The alternative view of African-American character, by mid-century, was a form of "romantic racialism," classically expressed in Harriet Beecher Stowe's *Uncle Tom's Cabin*. Even Stowe, however, saw African-Americans as fundamentally, and unalterably, different from whites—as childlike, innocent, and good-natured, qualities that white civilization had lost. Even such humanitarian liberals tended to believe, just as "Vindex," that colonization was in the best interest of blacks and that for their own good, African-Americans should be removed from an environment in which whites would always take advantage of their good nature.[49]

Whatever the intentions of nineteenth-century philosophers of race, the consequences of such attitudes toward African-Americans, coupled with demographic changes, included more violence on the streets of Lancaster beginning in the 1820s and 1830s. As Winthrop Jordan aptly put it, "the

Negro's color attained greatest significance not as a scientific problem but as a social fact." Even those whites who had once been supportive of blacks increasingly focused their humanitarian concerns on the local branch of Pennsylvania's Colonization Society, which had as its goal the exclusion of blacks from the community and their "repatriation" to Africa. As a result, blacks became even more isolated from whites among whom they lived and worked. They endured local and statewide attempts to exclude them from public places, as well as legislative efforts to expel them from the state.[50]

There were still white abolitionists in the county when Buley, Ford, and the two Hammonds arrived, and some of them worked diligently— attending meetings, giving speeches, and donating money to the cause. But for the most part, their efforts were aimed at the eradication of slavery and repeal of the Fugitive Slave Law, not the betterment of local conditions for African-Americans; on a day-to-day basis, Lancaster's blacks generally found themselves on their own. They still had white "friends," but African-Americans knew that if it came to a fight—as it increasingly did—it was a battle that blacks would have to fight on their own. So violence, isolation, and poverty drew blacks together. Their shared experiences, fears, and no doubt their dreams were the foundation upon which they built a community separate from whites. They had each other and their freedom (such as it was), and that counted for much.

What united Lancaster's whites across class, religious, moral, and political lines was a shared sense that African-Americans were aliens who worked in the region but were not truly members of the communities in which they lived. This vision of blacks as outsiders defined the limits of white tolerance, even among those considered "friends" of ex-slaves. It was possible to sympathize with the general plight of African-Americans, to give individual blacks some food, hire their labor to bring in the crops, pass on used clothing, and even harbor and assist fugitives from slavery without believing that blacks really belonged. Over time, as the numbers of African-Americans in Lancaster County increased and as they became more integrated into the local economy, they made claims to membership that enraged some local whites. And the violence that we see in the eighteenth-century court records now crossed racial lines perhaps more frequently, at least more visibly to us. It was in this new world of violent interracial relations, which grew from local cultures of violence established during the eighteenth century, that the four fugitives from Edward Gorsuch's farm lived for almost two years preceding the fall of 1851.

[3]

The Chase

1851 WAS A VERY BAD YEAR FOR FARMS from the Atlantic to the Mississippi. Unseasonably cold weather in the spring resulted in late plantings, which got everything off to a slow start. Then, throughout the summer, an almost unprecedented combination of heat and drought wilted crops in the fields and stunted their growth. The blazing sun baked and cracked the clay soil of northern Maryland and southeastern Pennsylvania. As August mercifully came to an end, it was clear that this season's corn, wheat, and tobacco crops would be two-thirds, or less, of the normal yield. When September began, farmers could only pray for some relief from the heat for themselves and their animals, a break in the weather that would give some hope for fall plantings. In early September, the topic for discussion whenever farmers met was rain—the lack of it, whether anyone could remember a worse summer, or prospects for a change. Conversation at Retreat Farm certainly included the weather, but the Gorsuches also talked about slaves, especially the four who were not there to suffer and work along with the rest.

Across the York Pike from Retreat Farm, to the east, was an inn that served as a meeting place for the area's white propertied class. Owners of large farms, doctors, lawyers, and even a liberal minister or two would stop for a drink, to exchange pleasantries, to discuss the weather or business transactions, or just to eat a good meal with family and friends. Located on land adjoining the extended Gorsuch family's other estate, Retirement Farm, the roadhouse was the largest in the area, and its proprietor was also, not surprisingly, a Gorsuch. Captain Joshua Gorsuch retired from his seafaring profession and built the hostelry in 1810. The brick building also housed a store, where country women could purchase imported fabrics, frocks, and hats and could browse among shawls, fans, perfumes, jewelry, teas, coffee, spices, and trinkets from around the world. The gentry also found imported liquors, snuff, watches, and sundries in addition to the commonplace domestic products sold by other local merchants.

Weary travelers knew the tavern for its fine food and drink, comfortable rooms, and the gracious hospitality of its host. As an additional service, the innkeeper provided accommodations for any slave traveling with the paying guests. There were cells with barred windows in the basement, where slaves could be securely locked for the night. This enabled the masters, who were perhaps on their way to or from the slave market in Baltimore or were simply on the road with a slave work crew, to dine at leisure and rest without concern for the loss of their human chattel.[1]

It was the matter of slaves that brought members of the Gorsuch clan together in Captain Joshua's tavern during the first week of September 1851—not the slaves in the basement, of course, or the slaves back at Edward Gorsuch's farm, but those who had run away almost two years before, at least three of whom had now been located in Lancaster County, Pennsylvania. None of the family doubted the informant's reliability. The "William M. P." who signed the letter of August 28 was William Padgett, a young man who, although born and raised in Lancaster, had lived for a time in the Baltimore area. Not exactly a family friend, as he had asserted in the letter, Padgett did know the Gorsuches, apparently recognized their escaped slaves on sight, and had assisted others in this sort of matter in the past.

Back in Lancaster, Padgett had a less savory reputation among those unsympathetic to the stalking of fugitive slaves. Local people later remembered him as a "miserable creature," who used his clock repairman's trade as a cloak for his labors as an informer. Once inside a customer's house, Padgett seized the opportunity to hunt out his unsuspecting victims. "During the fall months," a resident later recalled, "he pretended to be gathering sumac tops for the dyeing of morocco. By these means he became aware of every cow path and by-road, and could keep a close watch wherever he suspected a victim might be concealed and thus make an accurate report." Padgett reputedly had a talent for ingratiating himself with local blacks for the purpose of locating fugitives.[2]

Whatever the finer points of his personality, Padgett played an essential role in the attempt to recapture Gorsuch's slaves. He was also reputedly a member of the notorious "Gap Gang," a loosely organized band of working-class whites who terrorized the black community of Lancaster County. This gang of toughs took its name generally from the Gap Hills in the eastern part of the country, where many of them lived and worked, and specifically from the Gap Tavern, which served as a hangout and rendezvous for many of their endeavors. During the twelve months preceding September 1851, such kidnappers had used the Fugitive Slave Law as license for terrorist acts against black residents of the county. "Spies and informers were everywhere," a white Lancastrian recalled many years later:

> Every peaceful valley, as well as populous town, was infested with prowling kidnappers on the watch for their prey. . . . Quiet homes and peaceful communities were constantly threatened with midnight incursions of manhunters, with their treacheries, stratagems, their ruffian outrages and bloody violence, and menacing the defenseless people of color with a "reign of terror."[3]

The distinction between lawful and illegal attempts to capture black residents of Lancaster County was a subtle one, whose meaning was often lost on those unversed in the language of governments and courts. Illiteracy could leave a man more vulnerable to those who waved "legal papers" before his face, or it could make him wary of anyone who claimed to enforce the law. The authority of pistols and clubs could be comprehended by all, but weapons demanded quick, perhaps unreasoned, judgments in an atmosphere of violence and fear. So, in practical fact, the Fugitive Slave Law escalated a war between those who had tasted freedom and those who would try to deprive them of liberty's sustenance.

To the "kidnappers" of Lancaster County, the difference between a free black and a fugitive slave was often without meaning. African-Americans, especially men, were marketable commodities whatever their past and no matter what was the law of the land. To the black residents of the county, a kidnapper was a kidnapper, to be feared and resisted at whatever cost. These were the realities of life on the border between slavery and freedom; there were no laws in this war, except for the laws of nature that govern relations between hunter and hunted—the rules of survival and self-defense. Long after the Civil War, Josiah Pickle remembered one such kidnapping, which occurred on his father's farm:

> The Negro was a post and railer by trade and very industrious. One evening after dusk a couple of men in a wagon drove up to his house and asked his wife if John was home. She replied that he was not, but was working for a neighbor and probably was coming up the road. They drove away and met him, talked for a while, and one knocked him down and then threw him into the wagon when they drove rapidly away. A scream, when he was attacked, was the last that his wife and family ever

heard from him, and no doubt a large sum was received for him by his captors in some southern market.

According to David Forbes, who interviewed Pickle over forty years after the kidnapping occurred, "this is only one of the hundreds of such cases of the stealing of human beings at which the unscrupulous made a living, and there are several people still surviving, unless wrongly accused, who accumulated much of their wealth in this questionable manner."[4]

Skirmishes were frequent, with the hunters often seizing the advantages of surprise and darkness to pounce on their quarry. Kidnappers of the illegal variety succeeded in taking what the newspapers described as "an old colored man" in March 1851. In the middle of the night, the house was invaded by a party of whites who were unknown to the residents, displayed no warrants, and did not bother the courts with affidavits or testimony to the black man's status as a slave. According to the papers, "the old man and his wife made all the resistance they could, but were overpowered—the woman knocked down and the man captured."[5]

Earlier this same year, the legal capture of a fugitive slave in Columbia, Pennsylvania, provoked a riot. A farmer from Havre-de-Grace, Maryland, claimed the escaped slave named Stephen Bennett was his property. During the battle that ensued between lawmen and African-Americans who came to Bennett's assistance, the sheriff's arm was shattered by a bullet. Eventually, the constabulary assembled in sufficient numbers to recapture the fugitive and fight back the crowd. Residents raised seven hundred dollars—the asking price—to purchase Bennett's freedom, and the town settled back into a semblance of order.[6]

Those who were hunted responded in one of two ways to the threat posed by kidnappers and the new federal "kidnapping" law. Flight was the path of choice for countless hundreds, who decided that the odds were against them any place south of the Canadian border. The exodus of blacks from Lancaster County in the months surrounding adoption of the Fugitive Slave Law was described locally as a wave of emigration. Not all were sorry to see them go, but even the most virulent racists among the propertied white community had to admit that the cheap seasonal laborers would be missed by the local economy. Unbeknownst to Edward Gorsuch, at least one of his four escaped slaves had chosen this option months before the posse assembled at Captain Joshua's tavern.

Others, including either two or three of the fugitives from Gorsuch's farm, chose to stay and fight for their freedom, even if it meant death in the battle. The African-American residents of Lancaster County were not defenseless. They often gave as good or better than they got in this war for survival. They were not passive victims but a determined, self-led people who relied first and foremost on themselves for protection against those who threatened their liberty and their lives. All the blacks who remained in the county, somewhere in excess of three thousand souls, lived in fear; they worked, ate, prayed, played, loved, and slept in constant vigilance against the day that the kidnappers would come for them. Fear drove the black community even closer together than shared circumstances had bound them before. Two decades earlier they had formed a mutual protection association—a gang to combat the Gap Gang—which took an aggressive stance against all who threatened the life and liberty of any member of their community.[7]

William Parker led this self-defense organization. He was a man of courage, intelligence, bravado, and justifiable pride, who was admired by Lancaster's black residents, and some of its whites, and rightly feared by those who wished ill to him and his cause. By all accounts, Parker was a tall, thin, well-muscled mulatto man, whom his African-American neighbors knew as "the preacher" during his twelve years in Lancaster County. He was about twenty-nine years old in September 1851. According to a local historian, Parker had "a reputation among both the colored people and the kidnapping fraternity for undaunted boldness and remarkable power." He was the one above all others whom the slave catchers "wished to get rid of." A white abolitionist from the region remembered that Parker was as "bold as a lion, the kindest of men, and the most steadfast of friends." He was the sort of man who made an impression, even on those who met him only once. Parker "could have commanded an army had he been educated, and he challenged the universal respect of all of them who did not have occasion to fear him," another white man recalled. Local blacks "regarded him as their leader, their protector, their Moses, and their lawgiver all at once."[8]

Parker's life paralleled that of Frederick Douglass's in a number of ways. Parker, too, was born into Maryland bondage and secured his freedom by running away. Indeed, the two men had known each other as slaves; they were reacquainted in freedom; and later, in the fall of 1851, their paths would cross yet again. The violence of slavery had shaped Parker's nature, like Douglass's, at a tender age. "My rights at the fireplace were won by my child-fists," Parker would write in his memoirs; "my rights as a freeman were, under God, secured by my own right arm."[9]

Like the four fugitives from Edward Gorsuch's Baltimore County farm, Parker had a "good" master, who would not "allow his hands to be beaten or abused, as many slave-holders would." Although he was convinced of the evils of slavery, although the comparative lenity of his own enslavement bred the courage and imagination that persuaded him that he must be free, Parker, like Gorsuch's slaves, needed an impetus—an excuse—to propel him to freedom. Just as most others who ran away, Parker chose not to go alone; like the others, he ran away from a farm rather than the city and from a "good" master rather than a bad one. Unlike Gorsuch's slaves, Parker self-consciously created the event that "justified" running away:

> Much as I disliked my condition, I was ignorant enough to think that something besides the fact that I was a slave was necessary to exonerate me from blame in running away. A cross word, a blow, a good fright, anything, would do; it mattered not whence nor how it came. I told my brother Charles, who shared my confidence, to be ready; for the time was at hand when we should leave Old Maryland forever. I was only waiting for the first crooked word from my master.[10]

When the "crooked word" did not come, at least not in a timely fashion, Parker refused one day to work in the fields. When the master asked him why he did not labor with the others, the slave replied that it was raining, he was weary, and he did not want to work on that day. According to Parker, "he then picked up a stick used for an ox-gad, and said, if I did not go to work, he would whip me as sure as there was a God in heaven." The slave had succeeded in provoking his master, wounding his pride, challenging the system, and making the master look bad in the eyes of those who would see a black man setting his own hours in defiance of the master's rule. "Then he struck at me," Parker recalled; "but I caught the stick, and we grappled, and handled each other roughly for a time, when he called for assistance. He was badly hurt. I let go my hold, bade him good-bye, and ran for the woods." Parker was about sixteen years old at the time.[11]

Parker and his brother made their way north under cover of night, eventually crossing the Susquehannah River to Columbia, Lancaster County, Pennsylvania. Since they had grown up in the country, town life was of little appeal to the Parkers; so they sought agricultural employment. "Those were memorable days," Parker later recalled; he felt free as a bird; "instead of the darkness of slavery, my eyes were almost blinded by the light of freedom." The reality of life in the North soon intruded on Parker's idyll, and he found "by bitter experience, that to preserve my stolen liberty I must pay, unremittingly, an almost sleepless vigilance." The injustice of life in the North, the ubiquitous racism, and his status as prey of the economic system and of those who would try to return him to slavery were worth it, though, compared to the life he had escaped in Maryland:

> I thought of my fellow-servants left behind, bound in the chains of slavery,—and I was free! I thought that, if I had the power, they should soon be as free as I was; and I formed a resolution that I would assist in liberating every one within my reach at the risk of my life, and that I would devise some plan for their entire liberation. [12]

As Parker knew well, gaining freedom was one thing and keeping it another; helping one fugitive was a small step toward overthrowing the institution of slavery. But those were his goals, and Parker was not alone in his ambitions. One way to think about what Parker and his African-American compatriots were about in Lancaster County is to draw a parallel between the way that the black mutual-protection organization functioned in the early 1850s and the way that communities of escaped slaves, known as maroons, undermined slavery going back to the sixteenth century. [13] Like the maroons who lived in forests and swamps bordering the "civilized" South, Lancaster's blacks challenged the slave system by providing a visible alternative to the lives of northern Maryland's slaves. There was constant communication among blacks, slave and free, on either side of the Mason-Dixon Line; the Northerners provided aid and sustenance to those who ran away and engaged in guerrilla warfare against slave masters and their agents who dared to confront them in pitched battle. [14]

Eugene Genovese's explanation of the slave-maroon relationship and the function of maroons in undermining the slaveocracy applies in interesting ways to the interaction across Pennsylvania's southern border. The Commonwealth's free black communities served a transitional role in the history of slavery just at the time that Genovese finds the maroons' alliance with slaves suffering strain. Where the maroons were the obvious source of inspiration and aid for the slave who would be free during the seventeenth and into the eighteenth century, the free blacks of southern Pennsylvania served the same function for slaves such as Douglass, Parker, and the four fugitives from Gorsuch's farm during the antebellum decades. [15]

Power defined the differences between the ways that northern Maryland's slaves and the freemen of Lancaster County related to the injustice of slavery. "If a people, over a protracted period, find the odds against insurrection not merely long but virtually certain," Genovese reasoned, "then it will choose not to try." In light of such a calculation of risks, the boldest of Maryland's slaves ran away, while the bravest of Lancaster's

African-Americans stayed and fought. And, indeed, in numerous cases, those who chose flight while enslaved were the very same individuals who stood their ground under different circumstances; this was true for Parker and for at least two of the fugitives tracked by Gorsuch.[16]

The members of Lancaster's black self-protection society were no more attentive than the Gap Gang to distinctions between legal and illegal "kidnappings." "Whether the kidnappers were clothed with legal authority or not," Parker explained, "I did not care to inquire, as I never had faith in nor respect for the Fugitive-Slave Law." In part, such an attitude was reflexive. Since the Gap Gang did not abide by the law and since the white community suffered such lawlessness against the African-American residents of the county, the blacks did not enjoy the luxury of protection by sheriffs and judges. According to Parker, "the whites of that region were generally such negro-haters that it was a matter of no moment to them where fugitives were carried—whether to Lancaster, Harrisburg, or elsewhere." In light of such hostility, the blacks had to protect themselves as best they could—with guns and clubs rather than lawyers and writs.[17]

And defend themselves they did, in a series of ferocious battles, which resulted in bloodshed and death on both sides. In a riot outside the Lancaster jail, bricks, clubs, pistols, and fists were the weapons of choice in an unsuccessful attempt to free William Dorsey from the clutches of the law. On another occasion, the alarm was sounded that kidnappers were attempting to take a black girl back to Maryland. "The news soon reached me," Parker reported,

> and with six or seven others, I followed them. We proceeded with all speed to a place called the Gap-Hill, where we overtook them, and took the girl away. Then we beat the kidnappers, and let them go. We learned afterwards that they were all wounded badly, and that two of them died in Lancaster, and the other did not get home for some time. Only one of our men was hurt, and he had only a slight injury in the hand.[18]

The deaths of the two "kidnappers" were at least partly the consequence of the white community's attitudes toward such violence in the name of the law. As the slave-catching party retreated, they had a difficult time finding a local physician who would minister to the wounds of their injured members. "There are plenty of doctors South," across the Maryland line, they were told. "Men coming after such property ought to be killed," another unsympathetic white man lectured the posse. Ultimately, the slave catchers found sympathy and assistance at McKenzie's Tavern in Lancaster city. So incensed was the innkeeper to see the condition of the posse and to hear of their treatment by his fellow citizens, that he declared he would never hire another "nigger" and fired a black woman servant on the spot. For his efforts in the kidnappers' behalf and his public declamations of eagerness to extend hospitality to any slave owner passing through the town, McKenzie became the victim of arsonists, who burned his barn to the ground. The community was divided over the issue of fugitive slaves—bitterly, violently riven by issues of law and justice and race. This was a war, and it was not at all clear who was winning.[19]

The friends of the fugitives lost many battles; they frequently arrived on the scene too late to influence the outcome. Members of the self-protection society were not in time to save Henry Williams from being taken back to Maryland as a slave. They were also too late to help John Williams, who was so badly hurt resisting the Gap Gang that his master refused to pay the kidnappers when they arrived at his Maryland farm with their captive. Williams later died from head injuries suffered in the affray. Parker himself was shot in the ankle during one rescue attempt.[20]

Spies had a role to play in these battles. As in other wars, espionage was dangerous work and required anonymity to succeed. White men such as Padgett recognized that they had to be careful lest Parker's gang discover their betrayal. Parker saw the moral ambiguity, and the irony, of African-Americans resorting to lynch law in the name of justice, but the ends seemed to make the means "excusable, if not altogether justifiable," in handling spies. When they learned that Allen Williams had been betrayed by the black man in whose home the fugitive lived, the self-protection society stalked the Judas and gave him a merciless beating. When they heard that another African-American regularly assisted slave catchers in their bloody work, Parker's gang burned his house to the ground.[21]

Much of this violence occurred before the Fugitive Slave Law became the law of the land. If anything, though, the violence escalated in Lancaster County during the year following adoption of the Compromise of 1850. The new Fugitive Slave Law tipped the balance of power in the battle for freedom toward the slave catchers, as it brought federal law-enforcement officials into the fray on the side of the masters. It was definitely going to be easier to retake fugitive slaves legally. No longer could Pennsylvania's officials openly resist efforts to recover fugitives. No longer would masters be denied protection of the courts when they ventured north to recover their property. Despite several notorious examples of resistance, the law was being tolerated, even tacitly welcomed, in Pennsylvania, as in most other Northern states. According to Stanley W. Campbell, "for the most part . . . the law was enforced quietly and without fanfare." "By midsummer 1851," Campbell contends, "public acquiescence toward the Fugitive Slave Law was in fact becoming general." Some places in the North this was true, but not in Lancaster; Parker's self-protection association continued its work through the summer and into the fall of 1851.[22]

This, then, was the setting of suspicion, tension, hatred, and violence into which the Gorsuch party blundered. Lancaster County was not a vacuum, where all parties could be expected to engage in a reasoned dialogue that recognized the humanity of both sides. The fugitives and their sympathizers had learned to disdain the law that jeopardized their freedom. They had practiced the arts of guerrilla warfare and had gained confidence in their ability to fight. They had honed their hatred of slavery and slave owners, not just on their memories of life in Maryland but also on experiences defending their liberty in the North—against Northern white racists, against fellow African-Americans who regularly betrayed their racial brethren for the antebellum equivalent of Judas' thirty pieces of silver, and against the slave catchers who came from the South. A law, a piece of paper signed by a judge, and the bravado of a Southern gentleman would prove flimsy armor against the weapons of war.

In partial ignorance and in entire disdain for the realities of the slave-catching business—with or without the authority of a federal law—Edward Gorsuch; his son Dickinson; Captain Joshua, the aging innkeeper and a cousin of Edward's; Dr. Thomas Pearce, a nephew; and two neighbors, Nicholas Hutchins and Nathan Nelson, gathered their horses and rode away from the tavern.[23] Dickinson had tried to talk his father out of the enterprise, obviously to no avail. The old man was "determined to have his property" and would listen to no contrary advice. The stubbornness of the slave owner was again remarked on by his son—the unwillingness to listen to logic, to reason, or to measure his loss by any calculation other than his wounded pride. And so, Edward Gorsuch began the ride north to his death.

On September 8, 1851, Gorsuch took an express train to Philadelphia, arriving ahead of his party. On September 9, he secured four warrants authorizing capture of his slaves under the federal government's Fugitive Slave Law adopted the previous year. The fugitive-slave commissioner, Edward Ingraham, also instructed Henry H. Kline, the "notorious, lying, slave-catching Deputy Marshal Kline" as he was known in the anti-slavery press, to head the Gorsuch posse. Two other Philadelphia policemen joined up as deputies and were paid in advance by Gorsuch. Initially, the slave-catching expedition traveled in four separate groups for the purpose of making their arrival less conspicuous than it might otherwise be. Edward Gorsuch rode alone from Philadelphia; Marshall Kline made his way west first by train and then the rest of the way by rented wagon; the two police officers, John Agan and Thompson Tully, journeyed together on a later train; and the rest of the Gorsuch party came up from Baltimore, intending to join the posse at a tavern in Lancaster County.

Right from the start there were problems, which boded ill for the enterprise. Kline's wagon broke down, and he was forced to walk his horses back and hire another.[24] The delay caused Kline to miss the prearranged rendezvous, and he was left wandering about the Lancaster countryside conspicuously looking for the Gorsuches. Kline's cover story, that he was chasing horse thieves, was a transparent ruse.

Even worse, a black man named Samuel Williams followed him all day. Williams, who ran a Philadelphia tavern called the Bolivar House, was known by Kline to be active in the network of agents popularly known as the "Underground Railroad." Kline rightly suspected that Williams had knowledge of the warrants secured by Edward Gorsuch and was sent by the "Special Secret Committee" to warn Lancaster's black community what the marshal and his posse were up to. According to William Parker, Gorsuch had been noticed "in close converse with a certain member of the Philadelphia bar, who had lost the little reputation he ever had by continual dabbling in negro-catching, as well as by association with and support of the notorious Henry H. Kline, a professional kidnapper of the basest stamp."[25]

Having uncovered the slave-catching plot, it remained for Williams to discover what exactly the plans of the kidnappers from Maryland were and then to deliver a warning to those who were threatened. The Secret Committee knew that "one false step would jeopardize their own liberty, and very likely their lives. . . . They knew, too, that they were matched against the most desperate, daring, and brutal men in the kidnappers' ranks." This was not, according to Parker, just another slave-catching expedition like the hundreds of others that had gone before; this was one of the new federal "kidnapping" posses. The Secret Committee knew "that this was the deepest, the most thoroughly organized and best-planned project for man-catching that had been concocted since the infamous Fugitive Slave Law had gone into operation." Perhaps Parker romanticized the encounter for dramatic effect, but there can be no exaggeration of the danger into which Williams, the Philadelphia innkeeper, walked. Kline, who was by no means a brave man and who knew the dangers of the slave-catching business, was also scared. The Gorsuches had lost the element of surprise and thus their advantage, if the fugitives were found.[26]

At 2 a.m., Kline entered a Penningtonville tavern and inquired about the horse thieves. Williams, who had followed him through the door, responded to the inquiry with a clear threat: "I know the kind of horse thieves you are after. They are all gone; and you had better not go after them." When Kline left the bar, Williams was not far behind. The marshal stopped several times at taverns along the road to ask about the "thieves" he was tracking. He reached the Gap Tavern at about three in the morning, saw to his horses, and then went to bed. He got up at about 4:30 and rode to Parkesburg, where he found Agan and Tully asleep in a barroom. The two policemen told Kline where to find Gorsuch and after hearing how things were going informed the marshal that they were returning to Philadelphia. They, too, had seen Williams on the train that morning (before he got off and began following Kline) and suspected that he was following them. Williams had also seen the policemen and knew from the bulk under their jackets that they were heavily armed and up to no good. In light of the foul-ups and the abolitionist spy, the risks now outweighed their salaries in the judgment of the two mercenary cops.[27]

Kline proceeded without his deputies and found the Gorsuches at Sadsbury around 9 a.m. on September 10. Edward Gorsuch was angry with Kline for not making the rendezvous. True to his character, the embarrassed marshal lied and said that his wagon had broken because he had been driving fast to elude the abolitionist spy. In fact, Kline had not met up with Williams until after he had arrived at the tavern in Penningtonville on his second wagon. Gorsuch was also distraught to hear that the policemen intended to return to Philadelphia. Gorsuch and Kline headed off separately to intercept Agan and Tully before they left the area. The rest of the party was to wait at an agreed-upon place. When Kline found his deputies, they told him that they had already spoken to Gorsuch; now they refused to go with Kline. Agan told Kline that he had promised Gorsuch that he would return from Philadelphia on the evening train. The marshal and the Gorsuch party met the train that night, but neither Agan nor Tully got off any of the cars.

At about 1 a.m. on Thursday, September 11, the slave catchers left the Gap on foot and walked towards Christiana, where three of the escaped slaves were reputedly living. On their way, they were joined by a guide hired by Gorsuch for the purpose of conducting them to the fugitives. The guide disguised himself with a straw hat and bandanna to prevent his identification by those he intended to betray. Perhaps this was Padgett, the original informant; in any event, it was a white man who showed the posse the way.[28] First, the guide took them to a house where he said one of the fugitives lived. Gorsuch wanted to split up the posse, with a few of them staying to capture this fugitive while the others moved on to take the other two. Kline protested the foolishness of this proposed plan, pointing out that it would "take all the force" they had to capture the two other slaves. Finally, Gorsuch relented, deciding that since the escaped slave supposedly living in this first house had left a wife back in Maryland, he would probably be the easiest to take. They would leave the married slave alone for the moment and instead try to capture the other two. According to Marshal Kline, Gorsuch reasoned that "if he could see this colored man, the married one, [he] would come home of his own accord—he had been persuaded away; he [Gorsuch] then thought we should go after the other two." The master still persisted in believing, in the face of all evidence to the contrary, that his slaves would return with him to Maryland without any show of resistance, that the question would be settled by persuasion rather than force.[29]

The guide led the Gorsuch party another six or eight miles by a circuitous route, and then they halted briefly to eat some crackers and cheese, prime their weapons, and discuss a general plan of attack. A short time later, after having resumed their journey, Dr. Pearce stopped and was about to get himself a drink from the creek they were passing. "It won't do to stop, for it is daylight," cautioned the nervous Marshal Kline. No time to waste now, the new day was dawning, the fog that covered the valley was beginning to lift, and the slave catchers were about to lose the darkness and mist that shrouded their movements.

A short distance farther, the guide stopped and pointed to a short lane leading up to a stone house where he said the other two fugitives could be found (Figure 3.1). It was a small two-story stone structure with a shingle roof and a chimney at one end. There was also a rickety overhang above the front door. In the front, there were two windows upstairs and two more on either side of the entrance. To the left of the house, as a visitor faced it, was an orchard and then the creek that the posse had passed on their way from the Valley Road. To the right was a cornfield; the stalks were head high and parched from the heat and lack of moisture. There was a fence running from the creek around the orchard, parallel to the Long Lane in front of the house, and around the cornfield to the corner where the Long Lane intersected with Noble Road. Farther down the Long Lane to the northwest, past the orchard and the creek about a mile and a half away, was the residence of Levi Pownall, a Quaker farmer who rented the stone house to its occupants. A half mile in the other direction, around the corner to the southwest on the Noble Road, was the home of Castner Hanway, a white miller and the closest neighbor to the residents of the stone house.

FIGURE 3.1. The old riot house—William Parker's home *(with permission of the Lancaster County Historical Society)*

The setting was later described in some detail by a local resident with an eye for the strategic significance of the scene:

> This spot must have been an ideal one for seclusion, situated as it is near a fourth of a mile from any public highway, and standing well up on the northern slope of a hill, surrounded by trees, being almost invisible to the outside world, yet in such a position that the ever-alert resident could clearly scan the surrounding country for a long distance, and note the approach of suspicious characters in time to avert any impending danger to the inmates.[30]

The guide's job was now completed, and he walked away, leaving the posse standing in the Long Lane. It is at least possible that he had knowingly led the slave catchers into a trap. Whatever his intentions, circumstances were not exactly as they were represented to the Maryland "kidnapping" party. Whatever his goals, the guide delivered his employers as if on a platter to the very seat of Lancaster's anti-slavery resistance. Nowhere in the county would the posse have been more in danger for their very lives than on the doorstep of the stone house that was William Parker's home.

Inside the house there was at least as much nervousness about the impending encounter as there was out in the lane. The seven people who spent the previous night in the house anticipated the kidnappers' arrival. The warning brought by Samuel Williams had "spread through the vicinity like a fire in the prairies." Messengers crossed the countryside carrying the word, arming themselves and advising those of a like mind to be on the alert. According to Parker, when he returned home from work on Wednesday evening, September 10, Samuel Thompson and Joshua Kite were waiting for him. Also there that evening were Parker's wife, Eliza; Eliza's sister Hannah and her husband, Alexander Pinckney; and Abraham Johnson, a fugitive from Cecil County, Maryland, all of whom lived in the house. Thompson, Kite, and the rest of the household were in an uproar about the "rumor" concerning kidnappers. "I laughed at them," Parker recalled, "and said it was all talk. . . . They stopped for the night with us, and we went to bed as usual."[31]

Perhaps things were not so lighthearted as Parker remembered. Another account of that evening, based on Frederick Douglass's interviews with those in the house shortly after the riot, noted that the seven people "sat up late in apprehension of an attack, but finally went to bed, but sleep—they could not." Under the circumstances, with their lives and liberty at stake and without knowing when the kidnappers would pounce, Douglass's version seems more likely than Parker's. Sarah Pownall, Parker's neighbor from down the lane and the wife of his landlord, also stopped by that night. She wanted to share her concern about the possibility of violence and tried to convince Parker that,

> if the slave-holders should come, not to lead the colored people to resist the Fugitive Slave Law by force of arms, but to escape to Canada. He replied that if the laws protected colored men as they did white men, he too would be non-resistant and not fight, but would appeal to the laws. "But," said he, "the laws for personal protection are not made for us, and we are not bound to obey them. If a fight occurs I want the whites to keep away. They have a country and may obey the laws. But we have no country."[32]

Pacifism makes sense for whites, Parker responded to his Quaker neighbor; the law and the courts do not work for black people, and a man can run only so far. He was polite and appreciated her concern, but it was not her battle and certainly was his. Nothing more could be said between these two people who lived so close together but in such dissimilar worlds. They understood and respected each other but inhabited different spots on the long lane between slavery and freedom, injustice and justice, the law of nature and the rule of law. Parker and his African-American compatriots did not seek, did not need, and did not expect whites to come to their aid. Stay away, Parker advised Sarah Pownall, and try to see that other whites do the same.

One reason that the men whom Parker called Joshua Kite and Samuel Thompson were particularly worried that evening, and were even less likely to sleep than other occupants of the stone house, is because they were two of the fugitives from Gorsuch's farm. The moment they had been dreading, probably ever since they ran away from their northern Maryland enslavement, was now at hand—a confrontation with the "Master" in what could be a battle for their lives. At least they were armed, on their own turf, and in the company of friends who were brave and effective fighters for freedom.

Fear was certainly felt by the fugitives, but perhaps also exhilaration at the possibility of actually fighting for their liberty, of asserting their manhood against the very patriarch who had once ruled their lives. There were risks, to be sure, but this time they were not running away. They must have thought that they had a chance to win, an opportunity to strike a blow for freedom, an occasion to prove themselves equals of men who demeaned them and their race.

As the sun was rising outside, the posse, entering the short lane leading up to the house, startled a black man who was coming the other way. Imagine the emotions, the pounding hearts, the shock of recognition after almost two years, the adrenalin coursing through the bodies of them all. The black man was apparently Nelson Ford, one of the fugitives for whom Gorsuch had come. He had left Parker's house after that long, perhaps sleepless, night and was either on his way home (as Parker claimed) or serving as a lookout. According to an African-American resident of Christiana, who was interviewed many years later, Ford lived at the time in the house of Joseph Pownall and was known by the name of John Beard. The 1850 census lists Beard as a twenty-three-year-old black laborer, so the age and the occupation are just what we would expect. Gorsuch had used Ford as a teamster because he was small and incapable of the physical labors generally expected of field slaves. Beard—or Ford, or Kite (as Parker called him)—was also quick, eluded the slave catchers' grasp, and ran back into the house. "O William! kidnappers! kidnappers!" the young man cried as he burst through Parker's door.[33]

[4]

The Riot

WHAT HAPPENED UP TO THIS POINT in the story of the Christiana Riot is, if not obvious, at least pretty clear. It is possible with some sense of assurance to piece together the sequence of events. But from the moment that Joshua Kite ran back into William Parker's house, the narrative becomes significantly more difficult to reconstruct. The record is a contradictory jumble of individual perspectives, attempted self-vindications, faulty and incomplete recollections, bragging, and lies. Sorting out one version from another and recognizing each for what it is requires some tolerance for imprecision. In the end, the reader deserves a candid admission that even with the voluminous documentation surrounding this extraordinary event, we cannot be entirely certain of the sequence of actions, the precise dialogue, or the roles played by the major actors in the riot.

This is not surprising. Riots are by their very nature wild, confusing, and frightening experiences. Seldom does anyone have a clear perspective of all that goes on or the calm state of mind that contributes to rational perception and objective reporting. This riot was no exception. Chapter 7 will detail the specific testimonies given by some of the survivors; for now, my task is to provide a coherent narrative, which silently makes judgments about what happened during those first two hours after dawn on September 11, 1851, at William Parker's home.

When Joshua Kite burst through the door and delivered his breathless message, the first response of the inhabitants was to gather up weapons and climb the stairs to the top floor of the house. The second-story perspective gained the seven people—five men and two women—a clear advantage over the six men outside. In order to capture their quarry, the posse would have to ascend a narrow staircase one man at a time. The slave catchers could get no clear line of fire from the ground into the second-floor windows, while the Parkers, their relatives, and friends had the "kidnappers" within their sights.[1]

According to plan, four members of the posse staked out the corners of the house, so that none of the inhabitants could sneak through a back window or door. That left Marshal Kline and Edward Gorsuch to confront the blacks directly, to present the four warrants, explain the law, and take custody of the two fugitives whom they believed to be cowering upstairs. The front door was still open; the stairs were immediately inside.[2] The situation called for some courage, creativity, and good judgment. Gorsuch had the courage. Kline was creative, if nothing else.

The marshal called for the owner of the house. The imposing figure of William Parker appeared on the landing: "Who are you?"

"I am the United States Marshal," Kline replied.

"If you take another step," Parker warned, "I'll break your neck." Kline explained that he was there to arrest Gorsuch's slaves Nelson and Josh, that he had proper warrants and the authority of the United States government behind him. "I told him that I did not care for him nor the United States," Parker later recalled. Parker's brother-in-law was losing his nerve. "Where is the use of fighting," Alexander Pinckney asked his companions. "They will take us anyway." Kline heard the resignation in his voice and sought to encourage Pinckney's sense of hopelessness. "Yes, give up," the marshal responded, "for we can take you in any event." Parker tried to inspire his companions to fight to the death. "Yes," scoffed Kline, "I have heard many a negro talk as big as you, and then have taken him; and I'll take you."

"You have not taken me yet," Parker retorted.[3]

Eliza Parker grabbed a corn cutter, which she knew how to wield, and proclaimed that she would chop off the head of the first member of their band who tried to give up. She, too, was a fugitive from Maryland and had married her husband in Pennsylvania about five years before. Now at the age of twenty-one, she was the mother of three young children. Her mother, brothers, and sister were also fugitives, who lived in the Lancaster area. Indeed, Eliza's mother, Cassandra Harris, was helping to care for her two daughters' children, whom she had spirited away from the house temporarily to a safer locale. Eliza Parker and Hannah Pinckney were fighting not just for the fugitives from Gorsuch's farm but also for themselves, their families, and others who shared their fate. In this war against slavery, there were no black noncombatants. Women, children, and elder members of the African-American community were fair game; and anyone who could use a corn knife or corn cutter—implements known as well to women as to men—was a welcome addition to the line of defense.[4]

Gorsuch favored ascending the stairs to confront his slaves. The marshal told him to stop until after the warrants were announced. Kline proclaimed the contents of the official documents three times; from upstairs came the sound of bullets being loaded into guns. The marshal finished reading the warrants with a flourish of bravado—"Now, you see, we are commanded to take you, dead or alive; so you may as well give up at once." Then the two men began again to climb the stairs.[5]

On the way up, Gorsuch shouted to "Nelson" that he had seen him outside, had watched him run into the house, and knew that he was still there. He promised the fugitive that if he would come down peaceably and return to Maryland, he would be treated just as well as he was before the four slaves had run away. There was no point to resistance, the master explained, since he had the proper authority and the force to back it up. He would not leave the premises without his property.[6]

Someone threw a sharp metal object—apparently a five-pronged fish "gig"—at the two slave catchers, who were sufficiently startled to descend the stairs and go back outside. There was an exchange of views, perhaps a debate of sorts, between the occupants of the first and second stories on the meaning of law, the nature of property, the equality of races, and biblical justifications for the respective actions of the two sides. "Do you call a nigger my brother?" shouted the incredulous slave owner.

"Yes," came the chorus of replies from upstairs. A hymn resounded from the second floor:

> Leader, what do you say about the judgment day? I will die on the field of battle, die on the field of battle, with glory in my soul.[7]

Parker presented himself at the window and asked if he was one of the fugitives sought by the posse. Gorsuch, who was now directly below him, answered no. Parker asked his brother-in-law to stand before the window. "Is this one of your men?" Parker asked. No was the reply again. "Abraham Johnson I called next," Parker remembered, "but Gorsuch said he was not his man."

> The only plan left was to call both Pinckney and Johnson again, for had I called the others, he would have recognized them, for they were his slaves. Abraham Johnson said, "Does such a shrivelled up old slaveholder as you own such a nice, genteel young man as I am?" At this Gorsuch took offence.[8]

The ruse did not fool the posse. Kline threatened to burn down the house, pretended to send a message to Lancaster for another hundred men, and continued to assert his authority under the government and the law. Gorsuch again encouraged the fugitives to surrender, promising what seemed to him an irresistible deal, a return to the "mild" form of slavery they had experienced on his farm before running away. When there was no response from upstairs, Gorsuch lost his temper and threatened "Josh" and "Nelson" with harsh retribution. Dickinson Gorsuch was getting more nervous as time passed and his father's temper flared, and eventually pleaded with Edward to back away from the house. The son later recalled the exchange: "I told my father we had better go, for they intended to murder the whole of us. He said it would not do to give it up that way." Parker saw fear etched in their faces. The tension was clearly draining the old man, whose countenance had cooled from fiery red to ashen white.[9]

Upstairs, Parker's wife asked if she should blow the horn to bring friends to assist them. "It was a custom with us," Parker later explained, "when a horn was blown at an unusual hour, to proceed to the spot promptly to see what was the matter." Eliza Parker first went up to the garret and sounded the horn. The posse became visibly nervous about what it might mean and, according to Parker, began to fire on his wife as she trumpeted the alarm. She came back from the attic, knelt below the window where the shots could not reach her, rested the horn on the sill, and "blew blast after blast, while the shots poured thick and fast around her." According to her husband, the posse fired ten or twelve times.[10]

Shots were definitely exchanged. It is not clear exactly how the shooting started. Each side, not surprisingly, blamed the other for firing the first shot. Parker insisted that the posse fired first, when his wife began blowing the horn. According to one of Gorsuch's sons, who got the story secondhand from members of the posse, the inhabitants of the house started the shooting:

> While they [Edward Gorsuch and Kline] were on the steps and intending to proceed, one of the negroes struck at them with a staff, shod with sharp iron. My father then turned and went out the door. Just as he got out a gun was fired at his head from one of the windows, but the aim was too high. The marshal coming out right behind him, fired his pistol in the window.[11]

According to one account, the shot from the upstairs window passed within inches of Edward Gorsuch's head. The skirmishing continued. A metal projectile flew out of an upstairs window and caught Dr. Pearce above the right eye. Pearce shot back, but the pistol misfired. A piece of wood also thrown from the second-floor window struck Joshua Gorsuch on the shoulder, but nothing decisive was happening. The battle between the posse and the occupants of the house was a stand-off as the sun rose over the horizon.[12]

At this point, the slave catchers might have withdrawn in safety, perhaps to seek reinforcements or to fight another day under more favorable conditions. Dickinson Gorsuch, the slaveholder's son, clearly favored this option; Kline apparently agreed. "Don't ask them to give up," Dickinson pleaded with his father and the marshal, "make them do it. We have money, and can call men to take them. What is it that money won't buy?" The value of the slaves was not the issue either to young Gorsuch or to his father. They agreed that money was no object, but at this point the father's sense of honor would not permit him to leave the field of battle, even in a strategic withdrawal. "I will have my property or die in the attempt," the stubborn slave owner insisted. "My property I will have, or I'll breakfast in hell."[13]

Those inside the house wanted time to consider the posse's terms of surrender—"Josh" and "Nelson" turned over, the others to go free. They asked for ten or fifteen minutes to deliberate their fate. When the time was up, they asked for and were granted another five minutes. The posse believed that the fugitives were about to give up. Perhaps the carrot extended by Gorsuch was working—his promise to the two fugitives of no retribution and a return to the former conditions of their enslavement on his farm; or, maybe the posse's collection of sticks had struck fear into the blacks—the authority of the law, the threat to burn down the house, the fabricated note beckoning reinforcements from Lancaster. In retrospect, it looks as if the slave catchers were wrong, that they held out false hopes and misjudged the people upstairs. Those in the house were just stalling for time until friends could respond to the summons of the horn.[14]

Before the five minutes elapsed, people began arriving from every direction. Those inside the house saw Noah Buley, another of Gorsuch's escaped slaves, ride up on a gray horse, and more African-Americans were coming across the fields singly and in small groups. Almost all were armed, some with pistols, shot guns, or hunting rifles; others carried corn cutters, scythes, or other farm tools that would serve nicely as swords in hand-to-hand combat. At least one had a rock that he picked up en route. Zeke Thompson, called the "Indian negro," had a scythe in one hand and a revolver in the other.[15]

Not all the arrivals were black, and not all came on foot.[16] Castner Hanway, the white miller who lived right down the road, was among the first to arrive on his sturdy work horse. In retrospect, there seems nothing suspicious about Hanway's early arrival. He was the Parkers' closest neighbor, and he rode, while most of the others came from longer distances on foot. Not much information survives about the miller's life up to this point, because he led an ordinary existence and was not in the habit of recording his actions or thoughts.

We do know that Hanway had lived in the Christiana area for only a few months. A native of Delaware, his family had moved to Chester County, Pennsylvania, when he was five years old and then to Maryland for a while, before leaving for an unspecified western state. About three years prior to the riot, as a man in his early thirties, Hanway had returned to Chester County. There he married and then moved across the Lancaster County line to practice his trade as a miller. He was a man of no obvious distinction in life, who devoted most of his time to making a living and who was often covered with the white dust of his trade. If he went to church, we do not know which one. There is no record of how, or even whether, he voted; and if he had strong political views to this point in his life, either no one took note or Hanway kept them to himself. He had dark hair, which tended to curl on the sides and the top of his head, a receding hairline, and a beard (Figure 4.1). Nothing was extraordinary about Hanway, either physically or in the way that he lived his life. He was a quiet, unobtrusive man, who apparently got along well with his new neighbors, white and black. He seems to have been a good person, who had no ambitions to be great in the eyes of anybody else.[17]

That morning, Hanway was just sitting down to his breakfast, when his hired man informed him that Elijah Lewis was outside in the road. When Hanway came out and asked what was the matter, Lewis, who was a white storekeeper and the local postmaster, told him that "William Parker's house was surrounded by kidnappers, who were going to take him." Hanway went back inside, gulped down some food, and grabbed his straw hat. He was not feeling too well, so he decided to ride a horse rather than walk with Lewis the half mile to Parker's. Hanway was dressed that morning in the work clothes that marked his profession even to those who never saw the man before. "He looked like a miller," Marshal Kline would testify later.[18]

We do not know what was going through Hanway's mind as he rode down the lane that fronted Parker's house. It was not his fight, and he carried no weapons. Perhaps he hoped to mediate the dispute, to convince the blacks to desist from violence and the posse to withdraw before blood was shed. Possibly he was curious, wanted to check the slave catch-

F I G U R E 4.1. Castner Hanway *(with permission of the Lancaster County His-torical Society)*

ers' authority, or merely hoped to witness events as a check on the posse's behavior or in case any of the blacks got themselves in trouble.

In any event, Hanway arrived on the scene even before Lewis, who was making his way across the fields on foot. Lewis, just as Hanway, had started his day with nothing more in mind than plying his trade. Neither the shopkeeper nor the miller had plotted a confrontation at Parker's or had any advance warning of what was to come, although either or both may have heard the news about slave catchers delivered the previous day. Lewis himself was just opening the door of his shop, in ignorance of the unfolding drama, when an African-American farmer named Isaiah Clarkson came up and told him about the "kidnappers." The message was that they were trying to take Parker away, a misunderstanding of the actual circumstances. Clarkson insisted that Lewis must go with him "to see that justice was done." Lewis followed Clarkson, stopping first at Hanway's, which was on the way, then passing a black man named Jacob Woods. "Mr. Lewis came to me where I was working at," Woods later recalled; "I was just putting the chain to harrow; he said William Parker's house was surrounded by kidnappers, and it was no time to take up potatoes." So Lewis was recruiting supporters for the fugitives on his way to the scene.[19]

At the time, the appearance of the white men, first Hanway on his horse and then Lewis shortly behind, seemed to the posse more than a coincidence of timing. After all, on the heels of Hanway's arrival armed blacks were coming from every direction, emerging from the woods and the fields and walking down the lane. In the space of half an hour, there would be somewhere between seventy-five and a hundred and fifty black men and women on the scene, at least fifty of them with guns.[20] To the Gorsuches, who had a low opinion of African-Americans' intelligence and capacity for organizing themselves, Hanway was obviously the "leader" of Lancaster's resistance to the Fugitive Slave Law. "His presence inspired the blacks," J. S. Gorsuch reported a few days later; when Hanway arrived, "they immediately raised a shout, and became confirmed in their opposition."[21]

To the marshal, Hanway and Lewis initially seemed potential allies; after all, they were white like the posse, and the miscreants were black. When Kline saw the miller, he walked over to Hanway's horse and began to discuss the situation. The marshal's testimony on the contents of this conversation varied with each retelling and seems questionable in every version. Since Hanway never gave his account of the discussion, we have only the bits and pieces of what other people thought that they saw and heard in the midst of an increasingly riotous scene.[22]

All sources agree that Kline identified himself as a United States marshal and began to discuss the situation with Hanway when Lewis walked up. "This is the marshal," Hanway explained by way of introduction. Lewis asked if the lawman had shown him papers documenting the posse's authority. Hanway answered no. When Lewis asked, Kline produced the warrants, which Hanway read before passing them on. Lewis had left his eyeglasses at home, so he had trouble reading anything but the signature, which was larger than the type. "I saw the name of Edward D. Ingraham," the federal commissioner, Lewis later testified, "and took it for granted by that, that he had authority." According to Lewis,

> We had some conversation; he wanted us to assist in arresting somebody, I don't know who, and as near as I can recollect the reply of

Castner Hanway, he said he would have nothing to do with it, or something to that effect.[23]

Dr. Pearce, a member of the Gorsuch party, heard Hanway say to the
marshal, "You had better go home; you need not come here to make
arrests; you cannot do it." Pearce then heard the miller say something
that he could not entirely make out. "I could not hear that distinctly,"
Edward Gorsuch's nephew later testified, "except the word blood; the
marshal then told him he would hold him responsible."[24]

By this time a number of black men were milling around the three
whites. Lewis later remembered that the blacks had guns and threatened
to shoot the marshal and his men:

> Castner Hanway was sitting on his horse, and he beckoned with his arm
> (hand), "Don't shoot! Don't shoot! For God's sake, don't shoot!"

Hanway and Lewis certainly advised the marshal to leave with his posse
or blood would be shed; whether in the exact words remembered by
Pearce we cannot know for sure, any more than we can recover the tone
in which the advice was given. Pearce and the marshal remembered an
aggressive edge to the advice. Lewis recalled the circumstances and considered the warning an act of goodwill delivered by a very nervous miller,
who probably feared for his own life. According to Nathan Nelson, another member of the posse, "I said to him [Hanway] or he said to me
rather, that he didn't think we could do anything. I said I didn't think we
could. Those were the words as well as I can recollect."[25]

Kline was angry with the unarmed miller and shopkeeper for not helping to arrest the fugitives and told them they were committing a federal
crime by refusing to assist him. "I told him [Hanway], what the act of
Congress was as near as I could tell him," the marshal later testified in
court. "That any person aiding or abetting a fugitive slave, and resisting
an officer, the punishment was $1,000 damages for the slave, and I think
to the best of my knowledge imprisonment for five years." All the while
the white men were talking, African-Americans continued to arrive and
were nervously pacing up and down the lane, priming their weapons,
brandishing them in mock battle, actually pointing them at members of
the posse, and waiting for something to occur. After talking to the marshal, Hanway and Lewis explained the situation to several of the black
men standing in the lane, informing them that the warrants appeared to
be legal and that they would be making a mistake to resist the posse, and

advised them to disperse without shedding blood. "Don't shoot! Don't shoot!" another witness heard Hanway say again.[26]

Kline shouted to the rest of the posse that it was time to withdraw, explaining briefly that he would hold Hanway responsible for Gorsuch's "property." It is not clear exactly why the miller alone was fixed with blame rather than both Hanway and Lewis. Probably it was because Hanway got to Parker's first and arrived on a horse, evoking the sort of military image associated with being in charge. Kline called out to the Gorsuches, "come on now, your property is secured to you, provided this man is worth it." In other words, Edward Gorsuch could recoup the value of his fugitive slaves in a federal court, since the marshal would testify that the posse's inability to capture Nelson and Josh was a consequence of Hanway's refusal to help enforce the law. The miller would be liable to the limit of his financial worth for the value of the two slaves. Again, Kline misunderstood Edward Gorsuch's temperament, his reason for being at Parker's that day, and his refusal to leave the grounds even though the posse was now outnumbered by as much as ten or twenty to one. It was not money; it was honor, which could only be recovered by return of the slaves to his farm.[27]

Two of the Marylanders—apparently Nathan Nelson and Nicholas Hutchins—joined the marshal immediately. Dr. Pearce recognized that Edward Gorsuch had not heard, or at least not responded to, Kline's instructions: "I then went to my uncle and told him of the necessity of retiring, from the party outside not allowing us to make arrests." Pearce turned from the house and started toward the Long Lane with, he thought, his uncle right behind him. When he looked around a moment later, Pearce saw that Gorsuch had changed his mind and was headed back to Parker's house.[28]

People were running this way and that, shouting, gesticulating, but the crowd had no focus for its energy, which was still that of individuals rather than of a mob. The trigger that would unleash the anger at a distinct target was yet to be pulled. The rage was as palpable as the mist rising from the ground. Kline was mad at Hanway and Lewis; Gorsuch was furious with his fugitive slaves. Other members of the posse were angry at all of them—at Kline for his incompetence; at Lewis and Hanway, whom they assumed were abolitionist agitators, for refusing to help; and probably even at Edward Gorsuch, their kinsman and friend, for stubbornly refusing to acknowledge the danger faced by them all. The anger of Parker and the other blacks on the field had grown from a multitude of seeds—some of them planted in slavery and nurtured with whips and harsh words, many of them transplanted in the racist soil of the North by people who hoped for better than they got and received less than they deserved, and even a few seedlings of hatred fertilized on that very day by the slave catchers.

The catalyst for violence, the lightning bolt that started the riotous blaze, was a confrontation between Gorsuch and the man known in freedom as Samuel Thompson, one of the fugitives from his farm. Both men were angry by the time that Parker overheard part of their verbal exchange: "Old man, you had better go home to Maryland," said Samuel. "You had better give up, and come home with me," said Gorsuch. Thompson then knocked his former master on the side of the head with a pistol, which felled him to his knees. When the slave owner tried to rise from the ground, he was clubbed again, perhaps a couple of times. Thompson shot him once, then several others poured more bullets into the body, and in what by this time was probably a purely symbolic gesture, an unspecified number of participants whacked him across the top of the head with corn cutters, emulating the scalping of a fallen enemy from another cultural tradition of American violence.[29]

When Dickinson Gorsuch rushed to the aid of his father, someone struck the pistol from his hand with a club. Parker's brother-in-law then unloaded his shotgun at short range into the slave owner's son. Doctors later removed over seventy shot from young Gorsuch's right side and arm. According to the slave catchers' chronicler, by this time

> the negroes were whooping and yelling with savage glee over their victims, and the son, nephew and cousin started [running], to save their lives. . . . Dickinson, staggering under the stunning effects of his wounds, blood gushing from his mouth and streaming from his arm and side, took the southern end of the lane, and, in a distance of a hundred yards, reached the end of the wood, falling down by a large stump, exhausted.

Dickinson lay there for a considerable time, clinging to life by a thread. When he looked up, there was a white man standing over him, whom he asked to hold up his head. Although he made the request a number of times, the man did not touch him or make any move. Then Dickinson told the man he was thirsty and wanted a drink. "After asking him several times, he went and got me some water." At the time, young Gorsuch did not know the name of the man who silently helped him. Later, he identified Joseph Scarlett as the man. Parker said it was his landlord, Levi Pownall.[30]

In the heat of a riot, names, faces, facts, and sequences of events become a jumble. The actions of some are lost in the rush; others, who were surely not even there, are remembered clearly for their valor or cowardice in battle. Perhaps it was Pownall or Scarlett or somebody else who helped the wounded Marylander. In any event, it is fortunate that Dickinson Gorsuch got the water, because he was very badly hurt. By another account, some of the rioters followed young Gorsuch to his resting place, "but an old negro, who had been in the affray, threw himself over the body, and called upon them for God's sake to assist him, for he would die soon anyhow." So perhaps there were two samaritans—one white and one black.[31]

None who saw him in the hours immediately following the battle believed that Dickinson could possibly survive, with blood "gushing from his mouth and streaming from his side." Some "gentlemen" came and gently removed him to the Pownalls' house, where it was the opinion of an attending physician that the heir to Retreat Farm and Edward Gorsuch's slaves would not live through the night. But Dickinson lay there in a critical condition for a number of days. A week later, his brother would write that because of the charity of the people who owned the house, the good medical care of his physician, and the blessing of God, Dickinson still lived, "and we now have strong hopes of his recovery." It was three weeks and a day before the patient was strong enough to leave his bed (Figure 4.2). Between two and three months after suffering the wounds, Dickinson reported that "I have a pain in my side—it hurts me to take a long breath, and it hurts me very much to cough."[32]

When the shooting began, Elijah Lewis started down the lane toward the creek; Kline, behind him some distance, headed in the same direction. Kline caught up with Nicholas Hutchins and asked him to follow Lewis, to see where he went. All that the shopkeeper and Hutchins could see over the top of the cornfield was smoke from the shooting; all they could hear was the explosion of weapons and the shouts of the mob.[33]

Hanway was headed in the other direction. Why had Lewis and Hanway left as the shooting began? "Our object being accomplished," Lewis explained, "—to ascertain that there was authority there, we had no further business." Why did they not go back to assist those injured during the riot? "It is a hard question to answer," Lewis replied. Simply put, they were scared.[34]

After Dr. Pearce saw the apparently lifeless body of Edward Gorsuch on the ground, and after he witnessed the slave owner's son Dickinson being struck with a club and riddled with squirrel shot, Pearce elbowed his way through the crowd, jumped the fence, and ran down the lane toward Joshua Gorsuch, who was standing beside Hanway's horse. In the course of his escape from the mob, Pearce was shot at any number of

FIGURE 4.2. Dickinson Gorsuch *(with permission of the Lancaster County Historical Society)*

times. Later, he estimated that there were between twenty and thirty holes in his clothes; how many of these were from bullets and how many from scattershot he did not say. A pistol bullet had passed through his hat, luckily leaving only a scalp burn where it grazed his skull. Another bullet hit him squarely in the wrist, two more lodged in his spine, and a fifth in his shoulder blade.[35]

Joshua Gorsuch had also run for his life after seeing what the mob did to his cousin Edward. While he was watching the murder of his kinsman, someone beat Joshua over the head with a club. He fired his pistol in return, to what effect he could not tell. "All this time a thought flashed over my mind that I should run. I didn't have any idea of getting farther from where I stood, for I found they were determined to kill me. I ran, and they made after me," Joshua explained, in a still-muddled way, after the event. He ran even before Dickinson arrived to try to assist his father, passing him on the way without uttering a word:

> I jumped over into the lane then, threw my eyes both ways immediately and discovered on the right, a number of colored persons, and on the other side, some whites, but didn't notice who. I ran down, then, through the long lane, they hollering from behind me, "kill him," "kill him," and every one apparently that could get a lick at me, struck me. There was a man come riding by and I asked him to let me get up behind him. I said for God's sake don't let them kill me.[36]

Pearce, Joshua Gorsuch, and Hanway were all there together in the lane. Joshua was addled from so many blows to the head; Pearce was bleeding; and the three men were frightened by the bedlam around them. Pearce was trotting alongside the horse, trying to keep it between himself and a group of armed blacks on the other side of the lane; Joshua was running behind, trying to grab the tail or Hanway's leg to pull himself up behind the rider. And Hanway was just trying to get away without getting killed. The posse members were putting him in the line of fire.[37]

Hanway was a miller, not a warrior, not a hero, but an average man who was beside himself with fear. Pearce told people after the riot that Hanway used his horse to shield him from a group of rioters who pursued him down the lane. Hanway may have saved his life, Pearce told someone later that day. Parker remembered it the same way: Hanway "rode between the fugitive and the Doctor, to shield him. . . . if it had not been for Hanway, he would have been killed." Then one of the rioters chasing Pearce told Hanway to "get out of the way or he would forfeit his life." Hanway took the warning seriously and panicked, as many men would. Maybe he reasoned coldly that these slave catchers were not worth the risk. Whatever his thinking, if rational calculation was even involved, Hanway seized the reins of his horse, gave the animal a good kick in the ribs, and rode off at a gallop, leaving Pearce and Joshua Gorsuch in the lane to face their enemies alone.[38]

The two men continued to run down the lane, hotly pursued by a number of the rioters. As Pearce recounted the scene, "I ran with Joshua for a time, but finding that they were overtaking us rapidly, I ran off as quick as possible, and left Joshua behind." When he looked back, Pearce saw that the rioters had caught up with Joshua, and one of them was beating him over the head with a gun. Pearce made it safely to the field and continued on his way. Somehow Joshua also got away. Perhaps the rioters who caught him had run out of ammunition; possibly they had vented their anger and, mercifully, let the slave catcher get away. Parker's explanation for why the rioters did not kill more white men may be sufficient to explain Joshua's escape: "Our guns got bent and out of order. So damaged did they become, that we could shoot with but two or three of them. Samuel Thompson bent his gun on old Mr. Gorsuch so badly, that it was of no use to us."[39]

As Joshua, the retired sea captain and now innkeeper, wandered away from the scene, he had the good fortune to meet up with Kline. "I was knocked out of my mind," he later recalled. "He was as crazy as a bed bug," according to the marshal. Joshua thought he was within a few miles of home but could not find a familiar lane. Kline took the confused man by the arm and led him to within a mile of Penningtonville, where he got them both some water. This refreshed Joshua and helped restore his memory of where he was and what had just happened.[40]

The two slave catchers could find no one willing to help them. A man who initially agreed to take them into Penningtonville returned the dollar that he had accepted as payment and said that he had changed his mind. We cannot know whether his neighbors convinced the man that he had made a mistake trafficking with "kidnappers," or whether he realized that on his own. No one would help them find a doctor, rent them a horse, or give them a ride. So the two men walked to the next village, where the marshal put Joshua on a train. Relatives in York would take the man in and assist in the recovery of his health. It was fortunate for Joshua that he was wearing a heavy fur hat lined with handkerchiefs when the rioters beat him over the head. As it was, he would suffer headaches and other symptoms of brain damage long after the riot.[41]

Kline could find no doctor in Penningtonville willing to assist wounded members of the posse. He offered five dollars apiece to anyone who would fetch Edward Gorsuch from the riot scene. Finally, two men with a wagon agreed to run the errand, provided that Kline stayed behind. They feared for their safety if caught in the company of the slave-catching marshal. Kline hung out in the tavern for about an hour and a half until word got back to him that Gorsuch was dead and the body was being transported to Christiana for a coroner's inquest. The marshal attended the inquest, which he thought quite irregular because no testimony was taken and no one wanted to hear his account of the murder. Afterwards, Kline arranged for a coffin and shroud and had the body sent back to Maryland on the evening train.[42]

Some sources suggest that Edward Gorsuch was still alive a few minutes after the shooting ended. According to Parker, "the women put an end to him."[43] As the story was told in a number of versions, a sizable sum of money—in excess of three hundred dollars—was taken from the corpse and divided among the women who gathered in a circle around the slain "kidnapper." Several Northern papers reported that, after the riot, blacks had mutilated the corpse. According to Southern sources, the African-American women ceremoniously hacked the body to a bloody pulp with corn cutters before they were through. By at least one retelling, they even unbuttoned Gorsuch's trousers and chopped off his penis. This last detail was not reported in the papers, nor were the effects of mutilation described in official documents associated with the investigation and trial. The original source is not identifiable, but it was widely believed in the South. The governor of Maryland, for example, referred to the mutilation of Gorsuch's body in his annual address to the state legislature the following year. Although we cannot know whether the rumor is literally accurate, it is certain that the retelling rang true to those who clamored for judicial revenge.[44]

There is no questioning the larger truth, however, that black people organized and fought for their freedom at Eliza and William Parker's house that day. The warning of the slave catchers' arrival was delivered by a black man at the behest of a committee of black Philadelphians.[45] Other African-Americans spread the message throughout the countryside. It was the seven black people inside the Parkers' home who held off the posse, trumpeted the alarm, and refused to surrender. African-Americans, perhaps as many as a hundred or more, responded to the call, engaged the "kidnappers" in pitched battle, and won.

The African-Americans of Lancaster County were victims, to be sure—most were victims of poverty, ignorance, and lack of professional skills. Many were still victims of the slavery that they had escaped and of the law that supported claims against their freedom. All of them were victims of racism, which severely restricted their ability to rise above the social status that they endured.

None of the blacks at the Parkers' that morning were merely victims, though. They were not simply resigned to their fate—passive, depressed, incapable of challenging the injustice they suffered. Victimage was not their only status or their sole way of viewing their relationship with the wider world. They were capable people, courageous, and blessed with faith that the world could change for them and their children. They had vivid imaginations, which enabled them to envision a world different from the one they knew, unlike one that had ever existed in this country or, indeed, on the face of this earth. Not only could they picture a better world, but they were prepared to risk their lives, die if need be, to bring it about.

The character of African-Americans who lived in Lancaster County was not limited to the stereotypes portrayed in local newspapers. There were courageous fugitives who had the capacity for independent planning and action. There were free black men and women who rose above the squalor of poverty with honor, intelligence, and skill. These were the people who set the stage for challenges to the slave system. They were the ones who knew how to defend themselves when danger arose. To be sure, Lancaster's African-American community also had its share of cowards, drunks, and Judases. But what race or class of humans does not suffer the same misfortune? The story of the Christiana Riot and of the antebellum experience of Lancaster's black community is not solely, or even primarily, a story of cowardice, incapacitating depression, and betrayal. The African-Americans of Lancaster County were not merely victims of the injustices they endured. Sympathetic whites provided crucial, perhaps on occasion even indispensable, aid. But the blacks of the region were no more the tools of the white people who helped them than Joshua Hammond, Nelson Ford, and Noah Buley were the slaves of the corpse that was riding the rails back to Baltimore as the sun set on what had been a very bloody day.[46]

[5]

Aftermath

THE DAY AFTER THE CHRISTIANA RIOT was the hottest one in a very hot month. Thermometers in Philadelphia registered ninety-four degrees at 2 p.m. It was not only hot but also still incredibly dry; and September would be the driest month of the drought-plagued summer of 1851. The soil was parched; springs were unusually low; and the navigation of major rivers was, as one newspaper reported, "considerably impeded." Mills, such as Castner Hanway's, were forced to close part of the time for lack of water to propel the wheels. Farmers postponed sowing winter wheat and rye because of the lack of necessary moisture to germinate the seed, which would undoubtedly affect the size of next spring's crop. Pastures, too, the newspapers reported, "have ceased to be green; wells that have not before been known to fail are dry, and cattle are driven several miles for water."[1]

Leaves were falling prematurely; by the end of the month many trees were already bare. Worse yet, the heat of July and August was now replaced by conditions that were, for farmers, worse yet. September was a month of extremes, with records set for both high and low temperatures. Within the two-week period immediately following the riot, there was a swing of almost fifty degrees. Ice actually formed in some low-lying areas of the countryside.

Edward Gorsuch missed the record-setting heat of September 12 and the cold snap that followed on its heels. The last view he got of this world was of a parched landscape that looked, sounded, and smelled strikingly similar to home. The fugitives from his farm, along with the Parkers and Pinckneys, ran north as the leaves were falling from the trees. The last sensory perceptions of Lancaster County they had were of dry cornstalks rasping in the breeze, shorter by a full foot than they should have been at that time of year; of dust where there might have been mud; of brown instead of green vegetation. No, they would not harvest the crops that they had tended this year. They would not plant next spring's wheat and rye. They would not sleep another night in the stone house or walk again down the Long Lane to the creek. Their lives as fugitives would continue, on the run to another, safer, haven. Like Gorsuch, one of the last things they saw in Lancaster County was blood—the blood that literally ran from the "kidnapper's" body and that made small puddles, where in other Septembers rain might have gathered to soak the parched earth. At least figuratively, the blood was also on their hands.

The blood that was spilled on that hot September day in 1851 was the blood of white men. Several of the rioters were injured, but none very badly. Only two of the African-Americans required medical attention, which was furnished by Dr. Augustus Cain, a local physician sympathetic to their cause. "Of our party, only two were wounded," according to William Parker.

> One received a ball in his hand, near the wrist; but it only entered the skin, and he pushed it out with his thumb. Another received a ball in the fleshy part of his thigh, which had to be extracted; but neither of them were sick or crippled by the wounds.[2]

After consulting with family and friends, the fugitives from slavery and justice determined to split up into small groups. To his great sadness, William Parker decided that it was best to leave Eliza and their children behind for a while, at least until things quieted down. The children would slow the pace of escape, call unwanted attention to the group, and compromise the ability of the adults to defend themselves if confronted by bounty hunters on the road. Initially, a thousand dollars was offered for the capture of Parker; later he heard there was a two thousand dollar reward on the fugitives' heads.

So William struck out for Canada in the company of Alexander Pinckney and Abraham Johnson. The fugitives from Gorsuch's farm traveled separately, successfully eluding detection and making it safely to freedom. Parker's trio hid at a friend's house until 9 p.m. on the night of the riot.[3] They had a couple close brushes with posses at the beginning of their journey but then traveled the five hundred miles to Rochester, New York, without incident, part of the way on foot and the rest by a variety of public and private conveyances, including train and a horse-drawn coach.

The three men reached Rochester two days after leaving Lancaster

County and arrived simultaneously with the publication of stories about the riot and their escape in the New York newspapers. At Rochester, they landed on the doorstep of Frederick Douglass, Parker's acquaintance from their days as Maryland slaves. The fugitives were exhausted and dirty from their travels. After exchanging greetings with their host, they retired to wash the dust from themselves and their clothes. Before they were even done brushing out their hair, Parker and his traveling companions began receiving admirers who wanted to hear details about the riot and their escape. At last, mercifully, they were permitted to withdraw for some much-needed sleep. Then the host went to work in his guests' behalf. As Douglass recounted the scene in his autobiography, the three fugitives burdened him with a dangerous responsibility:

> The work of getting these men safely into Canada was a delicate one. They were not only fugitives from slavery but charged with murder, and officers were in pursuit of them. . . . The hours they spent at my house were therefore hours of anxiety as well as activity.[4]

Douglass asked a friend to travel the three miles to the Genesee River and inquire when the next steamer would depart for any destination in Canada. She returned with the good news that a ship would be leaving for Toronto that very day. "This fact, however, did not end my anxiety," Douglass recalled:

> There was danger that between my house and the landing or at the landing itself we might meet with trouble. Indeed the landing was the place where trouble was likely to occur if at all. As patiently as I could, I waited for the shades of night to come on, and then put the men in my "Democrat carriage," and started for the landing on the Genesee. It was an exciting ride, and somewhat speedy withal. We reached the boat at least fifteen minutes before the time of its departure, and that without remark or molestation. But those fifteen minutes seemed much longer than usual.[5]

Douglass remained on board until the last possible moment and then shook hands with the three men. As a token of appreciation, Parker presented his friend with the pistol that had fallen from the hand of a dying Edward Gorsuch. It was a "momento of the battle for liberty at Christiana," which Douglass greatly appreciated. In his eyes, the fugitives who were sailing off to new lives in Canada that night had, along with the rescuers of Jerry at Syracuse, inflicted fatal wounds on the fugitive slave bill. It became thereafter almost a dead letter, for slave-holders found that not only did it fail to put them in possession of their slaves, but that the attempt to enforce it brought odium upon themselves and weakened the slave system.[6]

According to this famous black abolitionist, "the thing which more than all else destroyed the fugitive law was the resistance made to it by the fugitives themselves." These three African-Americans and those who fought along with them had engaged in a battle for freedom comparable in significance to the Minute Men's engagement of British troops at Lexington and Concord over seventy-five years before. Like their predecessors in the War for Independence, Parker and the heroic black men and women who had fought at his side had won a signal victory in the war for the liberty of their race. These people were heroes in the eyes of many African-Americans and those sympathetic to their battle for freedom, not villains who should be jailed or executed for their violent deeds.[7]

Once the ship cast off from shore, the glow of the hero's welcome that they had received in Rochester quickly faded for the three fugitives, and the reality of their situation began to sink in. They had little money, no real plan for what to do next, no one to greet and guide them on their way. After reaching the Canadian shore and walking around Kingston hoping to see a friendly black face, Parker saw a man he had known back in Maryland as a slave. First, the man claimed not to recognize him, then succumbed to a sense of guilt, bought the three fugitives a meal, but did not invite them to his home. "How different the treatment received from this man," Parker recalled, "—himself an exile for the sake of liberty, and in its full enjoyment on free soil—and the self-sacrificing spirit of our Rochester colored brother, who made haste to welcome us to his ample home."[8]

It could have been lack of trust, lack of charity, or a failure of nerve that led Parker's acquaintance to leave the three men to fend for themselves. To be fair to the man, economic conditions were even worse for blacks in Canada than they were back in Lancaster County. The burden of three more people in need of help may just have been more than the man could bear. Perhaps Parker and his companions also reminded the man of a past that he was trying to forget; or maybe he was embarrassed by his less than "ample" house. It is possible, of course, that he was afraid to welcome the fugitives into his home—scared of lawmen; frightened by Parker, Pinckney, and Johnson themselves; or just plain reluctant to risk the little he had for yet three more among the thousands of African-Americans who were crossing the border to freedom. There was, after all, an attempt in progress to locate the murderers of Edward Gorsuch and extradite them back to the United States to be tried for their crime, so anyone who harbored the fugitives would be taking a risk.

In any event, it took the fugitives three weeks after they arrived in Toronto to find work that produced a meaningful income. "Sometimes we would secure a small job, worth two or three shillings, and sometimes a smaller one, worth not more than one shilling; and these not oftener than once or twice in a week." To add to his misery, Parker missed his family and had good reason to worry about their fate. For a month he received no answer to his letters but heard rumors about the capture of his wife.[9]

Back in Lancaster County, Eliza Parker, her mother, and other black residents also felt like anything but heroes. Eliza planned to make her way north with the children, to travel the back roads by night and hide her brood in haystacks and barns during the day, as her husband and his companions had done so successfully before her. According to her husband, she "had a very bad time. Twice they had her in custody; and, a third time, her young master came after her, which obliged her to flee before day, so that the children had to remain behind for the time." Cassandra Harris, Eliza's mother, was again called on to care for her three grandchildren.[10]

The strain was too much for the grandmother, whom everyone knew as Cassy. She was frightened by the violence, afraid for her family, sickened by the bloodshed, and unhappy with the trials that "freedom" brought into her life. By one account, she tried to convince her sons to turn themselves in after the riot, to return with her to the "master" whom they had fled in Maryland, and give up this hideous existence as fugitives in the North. The men tried to explain to their mother that, as bad as it was, they preferred their current condition to even the mildest form of slavery known in the South. They told their mother that as long as they drew breath, they had no intention of returning to Maryland as slaves. The sons then left her to make their escape, as did her sons-in-law Parker and Pinckney. When Cassy's daughters also left her behind to care for the small children, one of whom became extremely ill with the measles, the old woman apparently got very depressed.

According to some sources, the lawmen who swept down on Lancaster in a frantic attempt to capture Cassandra Harris's family tried, successfully it seems, to scare the poor grandmother to distraction. The white men swore in graphic detail that she and her children faced a certain death on the gallows unless the whole group surrendered to the law. The threats were obviously intended to extract information from Cassy about the location of her fugitive family. She very well may have tried to help

History Department

James Forten — John B. Russwurm
Edward Jones

David Walker

William Wells Brown

Charles Lenox Remond

Rev. Henry Highland Garnet

Lunsford Lane

Prince Saunders

Sojourner Truth

Frederick Douglass

History Department

Levi Coffin (Quaker)

John Fairfield (slave trader tale)

Harriet Tubman

Moral suasionist – Pel.

Elijah P. Lovejoy

W. Lloyd Garrison

Tappan brothers

Gerrit Smith

James G. Birney

Angelina Grimké –

Kansas at
Red Surt 1856
Lincoln Douglas Debate, 1857
Pres. elected of 1860

KUTZTOWN UNIVERSITY
1866

History

the lawmen in her emotionally disturbed state of mind, but she knew nothing about her children's places of hiding or the routes they were taking to escape from the country. Her daughters and sons had left her behind without the resources or information she needed to join them in their new life to the north. Perhaps she just needed to wait calmly and with a little patience until things were safe; but they had run away once before, when they left their mother in slavery, without telling her where or how to find them, and without so much as a word to ease her mind.

One newspaper said that federal officers arrested Cassy Harris; another reported that she turned herself in. One report described in vivid detail her experiences in Philadelphia after she was taken to the city by lawmen, was released on her own, and then begged Commissioner Ingraham and a federal marshal to help her return to her master. By a contradictory account, she never left Lancaster until a hearing before Commissioner Ingraham determined her fate. Either way, it is clear that the law had no regard for the welfare of the children in their grandmother's care.

According to the *Philadelphia Bulletin*, this thoroughly frightened and depressed woman was left to wander around the neighborhood of the federal courthouse in Philadelphia, apparently without funds or the means to get back to her grandchildren in Lancaster. If the story is true, it is possible to imagine some of the sources of Cassy's despair. She was a country woman from the South; almost certainly illiterate, she had seldom or never before been to the city and did not even have the price of a ticket had she been able to figure out how to get home. Her children were gone; she was far from home and deeply worried about her sick granddaughter.

As the *Bulletin* reported the story, Cassandra Harris walked up to the federal commissioner for fugitive slaves, whom she saw standing outside the courthouse on the corner of Seventh and Chestnut. She stood politely beside Commissioner Ingraham, who was talking with an acquaintance, and when he did not acknowledge her presence, she tapped him on the arm. Once she got Ingraham's attention, Harris said that she knew who he was and stated plainly that she wished to return to her master *immediately*, as she was "in a hurry." The commissioner was somewhat taken aback; no fugitive had ever asked to be enslaved, that was not a function the law and his authority were intended to accommodate. The idea was that blacks would be captured and brought to his hearing room by force. Once their identity was established to his satisfaction, despite their protests and denials, they would be involuntarily transported south.

If we can credit the *Bulletin*'s account, Ingraham must have been thoroughly baffled by this encounter. Harris's request was unprecedented in his experience and ran counter to all his knowledge of fugitive mentality. He probably thought that the old woman was a little bit off mentally, and that may even have been temporarily true. According to this newspaper, and others that reprinted the story, Ingraham explained to the woman that she would first have to find a federal marshal who would present her "case" in the usual way and, he might have added, ensure through proper procedure that the commissioner received his fee as called for in the Fugitive Slave Law. This had to be done formally and correctly, all according to the book. Harris was not to be put off easily and asked directions to the marshal's office, which she found and where she made the same demand.

A hearing was scheduled and held—whether at Cassy's request or by force, in Philadelphia or Lancaster, it is difficult to tell. Members of the Pennsylvania Abolition Society were present at the hearing to ensure the legality of the proceedings, and three attorneys served as counsel for the self-accused fugitive. Harris told her story in specific and credible detail. She was the slave of Mr. Albert Davis of Harford County, Maryland. About five years previously, she explained (it had actually been eight), on Easter day, her sons were given a holiday by their kindly master. Taking advantage of this lenity, the two young men ran north to Pennsylvania, where they were later joined by their sisters in what must have been a carefully planned escape. When the master found out about the betrayal, he blamed Cassy and said that she must have known what was going on and should have talked her children out of it or, failing that, informed him of the planned escape. He was sure that she must know the whereabouts of the fugitives, and when she insisted that she did not, he dismissed her from his farm and ordered her not to return without her children in tow.

Harris then hit the road north, a slave banished from her slavery, no longer wanted by a master who believed that the betrayal by her biological kin justified his anger at the woman who had nursed him and other children of the Davis family as well as her own. Since there is some dispute about her age—reported as either fifty-one or between sixty and seventy at the time of the riot—it is not certain whether young Master Davis dismissed Harris while she was still a productive working slave or after she had passed an age of real usefulness. Evidence from the 1850 census and the age of at least one of her daughters (Eliza was twenty-one) make it most likely that Cassandra Harris was about forty-three at the time she was ordered off the Davis farm, perhaps having just passed her child-bearing years and therefore of less value as a slave.

In the eyes of the master, a contract of trust and mutual interest was broken by the ungrateful young slaves, who did not appreciate his kindness and how good a life they led on his farm. Better to be done with the lot of them, he reasoned, than to keep the one whom he held responsible for the rest. Cassy Harris would find out the meaning of liberty for herself. The children would have to support themselves and their mother, and the whole family make their own way in the harsh winters of Northern freedom. The mother "kotched up" with her fugitive children in Lancaster County after a year of wandering about the countryside, begging for handouts, in search of the offspring who had left her behind. Now again after the riot, she told the white men in the hearing room, her children had deserted her, and she wanted to go back to the land of her birth.

A neighbor of the young master in question interviewed the fugitive and testified before the hearing that he recognized Harris and that he had established her identity beyond a doubt by asking for details about the Davis family and their Harford County farm. According to the master's representative, Davis had softened on the question of taking Harris back after hearing about her story and desire to return. He was now willing to find a place for her—not on his own farm but as a family nurse to another member of the Davis clan.

No other evidence of ownership was presented, no deed or will indicating that Harris's enslavement had passed from father to son. The testimony of the slave herself and of the master's friend from Harford County seemed *prima facie* evidence of her status and more than enough to satisfy the law. Generally, of course, Commissioner Ingraham dismissed the testimony of the alleged fugitives before him out-of-hand as self-interested and therefore totally unreliable. But this was a special case in any number of ways; a fugitive who wanted to give up her freedom was a political coup for friends of the Fugitive Slave Law, for defenders of the slave system, and for all those who hoped that the Compromise of 1850 would work.

Lawyers for the fugitive were also faced with an unfamiliar situation as the *Bulletin* reported the scene. They had to argue, contrary to their usual ineffective defense, that the accused fugitive lacked credibility because she was old, or confused, or a little bit off. They objected that no title had been proved and insisted that the father's will must be presented to the court. There was good reason to believe, according to defense counsel, that Cassandra Harris was manumitted upon the older man's death. Ingraham dismissed both motions as outrageous, declared the testimony conclusive and closed, and ordered the fugitive into the custody of the claimant.

In the abolitionist version—which took place in Lancaster, not Phila-delphia, after the arrest rather than the voluntary submission of a fugitive named Catherine Warner, not Cassandra Harris, who was fifty-one rather than in her sixties—there was yet another tragic twist to the story. A reporter for the *Liberator*, William Lloyd Garrison's radical periodical, wrote that he interviewed the fugitive in question after the hearing had determined her fate:

> She acknowledged that she had told the officers that she wished to go back, but said she was terrified by their violence and threats and feared a worse fate, if she refused to go. . . . "I thought I might as well go back as to live so. But now," said she with a wo-begone look, "I don't want to go back; O, I don't want to go back."

Harris made one last request of the commissioner; she would like the opportunity to visit her grandchildren to reassure herself of their well-being and that the sick one was returning to health. After cursory consid-eration, the white men determined that such a wish was, at best, an im-pertinence from a slave and an unnecessary inconvenience and expense to the man delegated to return her to slavery. This old woman was a pest, full of unreasonable expectations and demands. Never again would she see her grandchildren, daughters, or sons.

The young ones would eventually be reunited with their parents in Canada, where descendants of William and Eliza Parker still reside. As for Cassy the slave, she would live the rest of her life back in Maryland, how much happier or despondent in slavery than she had been in free-dom we simply do not know. We can suspect that she missed her family, but perhaps she was angry with them, as well—for worrying her so and leaving her twice to her own devices in old age. There were no pensions for slaves or for agricultural laborers in the North. Did her children in-clude her in their plans; would they have sent for her in due course if she had just been a little more patient? Was she even fit for the journey or the new life so much farther to the cold north? Cassandra Harris may have thought in one way or another about all of these things, but her feelings are left to our limited abilities to picture ourselves in her place.

Maybe Harris never really comprehended the meaning of freedom, having lost at a younger age the spark that gives liberty its glow. To be black and on their own in the North was both a blessing and a trial for her children; for the old woman the blessing was more difficult to see.

The Christiana Riot was possibly more tragic for this slave than it was for the Gorsuches, who lost one member of their family while she lost them all.[11]

Cassandra Harris was not the only one who was scared in the aftermath of the riot, and she was not alone in her wish for the comparative security of slavery as opposed to a noose or a jail. Abraham Hall made a similar plea when he was arrested several days after the riot. He had always been a particular favorite of his master, Hall told his captors, but he had run away from Maryland in 1847 out of fear of punishment for hurting his master's grandson. After four years he hoped that tempers had cooled; in any event, accepting the whip that might greet him was preferable to facing the "reign of terror" that followed the riot in Lancaster County.[12]

In point of fact, Hall explained, he had tried several times in the past to return to his Maryland enslavement but was prevented by neighbors and friends. He never said what form this "prevention" took but implied that more than gentle persuasion was involved. Hall's testimony provided more copy for newspapers sympathetic to the interests of slave owners. According to the pro-slavery writers who reported this case, there was reason to believe that fugitive slaves were being kept by force in the North, no doubt by unscrupulous capitalist entrepreneurs who held "free" blacks in wage bondage, while hypocritically and self-interestedly agitating for the abolition of the competing slave system, which was actually more humane to its workers, as the experiences of Harris and Hall pointed out. Many slave owners continued to believe, just as had the late Edward Gorsuch, that if the fugitives had a choice, the opportunity, and full information rather than the lies fed them instead of food by Northern abolitionists, the escaped slaves would really want to come home.[13]

With the possible exceptions of Harris and Hall, the fugitives swept up in the wake of the riot were anything but eager to return to the status of slaves. Another of the tragedies resulting from the Christiana Riot was the opportunity it presented for wholesale arrests of fugitive slaves. As one anti-slavery newspaper reported with both sadness and anger:

> When we saw the horde that, in the name of law, were the other day poured upon Lancaster county, and witnessed the ferocity with which they pursued and indiscriminately seized colored men, whether implicated or not in the Gorsuch affray, we felt assured that one prominent motive of that search with many engaged in it, was the capture of fugitive slaves, and the result is already sadly confirming that conviction.

Under the guise of seeking out and arresting rioters responsible for the murder of Edward Gorsuch, another Philadelphia periodical claimed, authorities were trying to "excite to greater intensity the already existing unjust and cruel prejudice against the colored inhabitants of the State."[14]

During the two weeks after the riot, for example, a free African-American living in the same area was captured by a Maryland slave-hunting gang. The man was released when resistance seemed to threaten the kidnappers' lives. Fugitives from Virginia engaged in a ferocious battle with those who pursued them, resulting in the serious injury of several white men and the death of at least one. Two of the fugitives apparently escaped, while two more were captured and incarcerated in a Virginia jail until they could be tried and executed for insurrection and murder. Closer to Lancaster, four African-Americans were taken and held in jail on the accusation that they were Edward Gorsuch's escaped slaves by slave catchers who knew they were not. The ruse was designed to buy time while the real owners of the fugitives could be notified by telegraph and travel north with their legal claims to ownership of the four men. Despite protests by outraged opponents of the Fugitive Slave Law, the men were returned to their masters, and it was determined that the falsehood had broken no law.[15]

Whether these and other encounters like them were "caused" by the Christiana Riot or were simply products of the slave-catching business as usual is difficult to say. Clearly though, every "kidnapping" episode would now be reported and analyzed in light of the riot. The battle at the Parkers' became a lens through which the expectations of all sides in the slave-catching controversy would be seen. It was even more difficult after the riot for Southern masters to suppress the reality of their slaves' attitudes toward enslavement and their willingness to engage in violence under circumstances favorable to their triumph. It was also less likely that fugitive slaves and free blacks would believe they were "safe" in the North, that the law and the white population protected them from those who threatened their liberties and their lives. In these senses, the riot did contribute to the atmosphere of violence that surrounded race relations during the 1850s; but before the prosecution of any Christiana rioters, the consequences of violence for those who survived the immediate battle were not entirely clear.

In Lancaster itself, a posse of about fifty locals was assembled by 10 p.m. on the night following the riot and was supplemented over the course of the evening by "gangs of armed ruffians" from Maryland, who were even more eager to vent their anger over Gorsuch's death on the black and white citizens of Lancaster County. "Wo to them who resist!" was the motto of this outraged assemblage of white men from Baltimore and Lancaster County and an accurate reflection of the thirst for revenge that would inspire their actions over the next couple of days. Working-class whites, who had no fondness for the African-American laborers who competed with them for jobs, were amply represented in this group. Almost all of the forty Irish railroad workers employed in the county were deputized, and one of them, when he was handed a horse pistol for the job, declared enthusiastically that he would shoot "the first black thing" he saw, even if it was a cow. According to David R. Forbes, a local chronicler of the riot:

> there never went unhung a gang of more depraved wretches and desperate scoundrels than some of the men employed as "officers of the law" to ravage this country and ransack private houses in the man-hunt which followed the affray.

Indeed, among the new deputies were two men who had done time in the penitentiary for breaking and entering the mayor's office, one of whom had since been indicted on several occasions for stealing chickens. These were the "lawmen" sent out to capture African-American criminals who had fought for their freedom.[16]

Independently of local authorities, federal officials made their own plans to capture those responsible for violent resistance to the Fugitive Slave Law. A contingent of about forty-five marines and a detachment of about forty Philadelphia policemen swept down on this rural community in pursuit of the same men sought by local officials. When a bystander asked what they were up to, one of the marines responded that "We are going to arrest every nigger and damned abolitionist" in the county. True to their word, the troops scoured the countryside in a mad attempt to arrest every black person they could find. A controversy arose about who had primary jurisdiction over the prisoners and whether they would be held and tried locally for murder or taken to Philadelphia to face federal treason charges. The parties reached an agreement that each would make its own arrests.[17]

Both posses hunted fugitives with little regard for the constitutional rights of the citizenry; nor were the deputized laborers, policemen, and marines attentive to which members of the community they captured or how much violence they used to make an arrest. African-Americans were fair game for those who sought to even a score, act out their racial bigotry, or who just enjoyed bashing heads. According to one witness, blacks were "hunted like partridges" by those deputized for the search. A brief "reign of terror" ensued, in which, according to a local historian, "whites and blacks, bond and free, were rather roughly handled; few households in the region searched were safe from rude intrusion; many suffered terrifying scenes and sounds."[18]

Peter Woods, a black man who was seventeen at the time of the riot, later told of his own arrest and that of his white employer, Joseph Scarlett, two days after Edward Gorsuch was killed. "When Scarlet[t] was arrested," Woods recalled,

> they were rough in arresting him. They took him by the throat, and pointed bayonets at him all around him. I said to myself if you arrest a white man like that, I wonder what you will do to a black boy? . . . I was plowing or working the ground, and when I saw the officers come to make the arrests, I quickly got unhitched and went towards Bushong's, and soon there was six of us together and we went to Dr. Dingee's graveyard and hid. . . . Then they got us. . . . The man with the mace, the marshal I guess, said "I got a warrant for Peter Woods." They pointed me out and then he struck me and took me up a flight of stairs, and then they tied me. Then they started away with me and tried to get me over a fence. They had me tied around my legs and around my breast, and they put me in a buggy and took me to Christiana.[19]

Warrants were issued for five white men in addition to dozens of blacks. Elijah Lewis and Castner Hanway rode into Lancaster city when they heard they were wanted and surrendered to the authorities, who were using Frederick Zercher's hotel as their temporary headquarters. The two white men were wise to deliver themselves into the hands of the law before one or both of the posses descended on their homes to drag them both in. Emotions ran high, and the deputies were not in the mood to be gentle or fair.

As Hanway and Lewis stepped onto the porch of the hotel, Marshal Kline approached them in a menacing manner. "You white-livered scoundrels . . . ," Kline addressed the two men with his fists clenched, "when I plead[ed] for my life like a dog and begged you not to let the blacks fire upon us, you turned round and told them to do so." According to witnesses, Lewis responded, "No, I didn't"; but Hanway had nothing to say. Lancaster Alderman J. Franklin Reigart, who would be taking preliminary testimony that day, grabbed Kline by the shoulder to restrain him and insisted that the marshal's behavior was out of place. "I hope you will say nothing to produce a disturbance," Reigart declared, "we wish to do our business legally and in order." Kline apologized and expressed his intention to obey the directive but explained that it was impossible for him to suppress his feelings after the events of the previous day.[20]

There was so much hostility against Lewis and Hanway among those gathered at the hotel that Reigart feared Kline would inspire a serious disturbance. A lynch party composed of the posse was not an unreasonable fear. Much more of the anger over Gorsuch's murder was aimed at the two white men than at the blacks who perpetrated the act. "Against the black persons [brought in by the posse for questioning] nothing was said," Alderman Reigart later remembered; "they seemed much enraged against Hanway and Lewis." On the scene, as elsewhere in the nation, when those unsympathetic to the cause of fugitive slaves learned details of the riot, they saw Hanway and Lewis as the leaders and primarily to blame for the resistance to Kline's posse, Edward Gorsuch's death, and the escape of those fugitive slaves who murdered the Maryland farmer.[21]

Testimony against those captured by the posses continued all day and into the night on the Saturday, Sunday, and Monday following the riot. The hearings at Christiana were brought to a close on Monday at 10 p.m. The local officials had the first crack at the prisoners, but now the federal prosecutors wanted to begin to prepare their treason case. On September 23, 1851, the hearings would resume under federal auspices in Lancaster city at the county courthouse. The principal witnesses against the accused were Marshal Kline and a black drifter named George Washington Harvey Scott. Kline's testimony was clearly aimed at self-vindication and given out of a desire for revenge, in addition to his dedication to enforcing the law. He was being accused of cowardice on the field of battle; rumor had it that the Gorsuch party blamed him for foolishly leading them into a trap and then deserting his posse when the bullets started to fly.

In Kline's first official telling of the riot story that day, Hanway and Lewis were actors, but not "leaders" of the violence per se. They refused to assist the posse and appeared to counsel with the blacks before the violence began. Kline remembered Joseph Scarlett riding up very fast on a sweating horse. "You have been the man giving the negroes information," the marshal recalled saying to Scarlett, who made no reply. So the three whites were certainly blameworthy, guilty of a serious crime, but as yet not the organizers and leaders of violence as they would eventually be portrayed. It was Dr. Pearce, another member of the Gorsuch posse, who first suggested that the blacks in the house were inspired to resist by Hanway's arrival.[22]

Perhaps Pearce's account rang true with the marshal when he first heard it in the courtroom that day. It gave the story a focus and placed blame even more squarely on the shoulders of a man they actually had in custody rather than on Parker and the others who got away. Possibly, the notion of white leadership first suggested by the Southerner accorded with Kline's own views of the role played by white abolitionists in orchestrating resistance to the Fugitive Slave Law. In any event, it was a version that Kline would remember, retell, and embellish in another courtroom on another day.

Counsel for the accused tried to poke holes in the marshal's story, as it was their job to do. Where was he when the murder of Edward Gorsuch occurred? How much of the violence did Kline actually witness, and how much did he just hear and piece together while hiding in a field of dried-out corn? "When I saw the negroes pointing their guns at me I got over the fence into the cornfield," the marshal admitted under cross-examination by Thaddeus Stevens, congressman, abolitionist, and now principal counsel to Hanway and Lewis. Was it not remarkable that Kline was able to see so much and with such clarity from his vantage and on such a foggy morning as he described? How could he identify by name and with such precision black men whom he only glimpsed, at best, and had never seen before? How did he explain the contradictions in his story and the different versions that he had told over the previous couple of days?[23]

The prosecution's other main witness at these hearings claimed to have watched the riot as an unarmed bystander. Harvey Scott provided the names of black men whom he said were actively engaged in the mayhem, and his testimony accorded in every regard with Marshal Kline's. John Morgan, Henry Simms, and William Brown were there, according to Scott. And he also saw the white miller Hanway walking around. Simms shot Edward Gorsuch, and Morgan slashed him on the head with a corn cutter, just as Kline said. Scott said he saw Brown, whom Kline had accused of being among the most violent rioters, at Parker's with a gun. At this, Brown confronted the witness: "Did you see me there George?"

"I saw you there," Scott insisted, "in the yard, pretty soon in the morning."[24]

Neither Dr. Pearce nor Nicholas Hutchins was as useful to the prosecution as Scott and Kline. "I can't say that I recognize those black prisoners," Pearce testified under oath. "I think I saw that large black man Morgan standing near the bars, with a club in his hand," Hutchins tentatively observed after gazing intently at the line-up of black men and women brought into court. The local constable and another of the Parkers' neighbors did not reach the riot scene until after the firing had ceased and thus were unable to link any specific prisoner with any particular crime. The prosecution located several more local people who were able